WHAT PEOPLE ARE SAYING

YOU TOO CAN BE DEBT FREE will be a huge help to everyone who is intentional about their finances, not only to the person who is in debt but also to the person who does not want to be in debt. Debt management is a very common financial issue and this book is not the typical book in any way because it provides you with ACTIONABLE steps to take when in debt, how to pay off and also how to avoid the cycle of debt.

I will describe this book as a must-have to everyone who is serious about their finances, not just to get out of the debt but it will help not to even get into debt. It is simply a goldmine for debt management. I love that it is faith-themed with quotes and Bible verses. I love that this book acknowledges that God is interested in our financial wellbeing."

Mercy Agbeti
Financial Literacy Influencer

As someone who has dealt with the consequences of bad financial decisions that resulted in a humongous amount of debt, Chris's recount of his personal experiences in his book brought back many painful memories. The braveness that it takes to put pen to paper in such a vulnerable way is laudable. Some of the events will sound like a scene out of the mind of a creative scriptwriter, but I assure you they are true events, lived by my friend Chris and thousands, even hundreds of thousands of others struggling with debt. That being said, "You Too Can Get Out of Debt" is written in such a relatable way that you will feel as if you are living the experience with Chris, even if you haven't experienced debt before. This book is packed full of lessons that will serve as a guide for you if you are going through the debt cycle and will serve as a note of caution to avoid debt if you are among those fortunate not to have borrowed or owed before. This is definitely a recommendation from me to grab a copy for yourself and everyone in your circle.

Titilope Ibilola
Author, Zero Balance
Founder, The Zero Debt Network

Chris Omoijiade's book eloquently addresses the concept of achieving debt freedom in a straightforward yet engaging way. It offers a well-rounded perspective that combines logic, spirituality, and practicality on attaining financial freedom, regardless of the current debt amount. I wholeheartedly suggest giving it a read.

Seyi Abiodun
Certified Financial Education Instructor
Coach & Business Consultant

YOU TOO CAN BE DEBT FREE

Also by Chris Omoijiade

SO YOU WANT TO LEAD

THE IRREFUTABLE ROLE OF
GATEKEEPERS TO YOUR SUCCESS
AND KEY PRINCIPLES ON HOW
TO WIN THEM OVER

LEADERSHIP GEMS IN THE BIBLE:
(The Old Testament Volume 1)

LEADERSHIP GEMS IN THE BIBLE:
(The Old Testament Volume 2)

LEADERSHIP GEMS IN THE BIBLE:
(The New Testament)

GET AHEAD: Practical Steps To Face Life's
Realities and Embrace Success

YOU TOO CAN BE

A FIRSTHAND WITNESS ACCOUNT OF THE HORRORS OF DEBT

DEBT FREE

CHRIS OMOIJIADE

YOU TOO CAN BE DEBT-FREE

Furthermore, the publisher does not have control over and does not assume any responsibility for author or third-party websites or their content.

unless otherwise indicated, all Scripture quotations were taking from THE KING JAMES VERSION of the Bible.

Scripture quotations noted NIV are from The Holy Bible, NEW INTERNATION VERSION.

Scripture quotations noted NLT are from The Holy Bible, NEW LIVING TRANSLATION.

Scripture quotations noted ESV are from The Holy Bible, ENGLISH STANDARD VERSION.

Published by:
ScribeTribe Africa
5, Prince Ibrahim Eletu Avenue,
Lekki, Lagos

www.scribetribe.media
scribetribeafrica@gmail.com
+234 (0) 708 040 1080, +234 (0) 813 527 3602

Distributed by:
The Chris Omoijiade Company
+234 810 950 0000, +234 908 123 0000
ceo@tcocglobal.com
admin@tcocglobal.com
www.tcocglobal.com
chrisomoijiade
Chris Omoijiade
Christopher Omoijiade
Christopher Omoijiade

THE
Chris Omoijiade
COMPANY
SOLI DEO GLORIA

CHRISTOPHER E. OMOIJIADE
SOLI DEO GLORIA

ARIMATHEA
ARIMATHEA BELIEVERS NETWORK

*This book is dedicated to Yahweh,
the I Am, the Holy Father of all spirits
and heavenly lights*

*To Jesus the Christ, Prince of Peace,
the Word and Eternal King*

*And the indispensable
Sceptre of the living Sovereign God,
Spirit of Glory, Wisdom, and Revelation,
the Holy Spirit.*

*I am indeed a product of
undeserved mercy.*

*Thank you, Abba, for
adopting me!*

THANK YOU!

To my wife, Oduola, for standing with me through the tough periods and embarrassing episodes. For radiating enough hope and respite that saw me through the black hole of debt, which literally threatened to permanently quench my light and crush my spirit. For forgiving my errors, providing when I couldn't, and most importantly, for always believing that I am destined for the top, even at moments I when stopped believing in myself. Thank you to my amazing sons, Christopher (III) and Ethan; you were the bright stars that illumined those seemingly endless, very dark nights. To my parents, Prince and Mrs C. J. Omoijiade, pillars in a season of darkness.

THE 'WHY' BEHIND THIS BOOK

---

*"Praise be to the God and Father of our Lord Jesus Christ, the Father of compassion and the God of all comfort, who comforts us in all our troubles, **so that we can comfort those in any trouble with the comfort we ourselves receive from God.**"*
- 2 Corinthians 1:3-4 (NIV)

My prayer is that through this book I can comfort you; from that which I have also undeservedly received. You don't have to experience my story but it can participate in your life, and place a huge chasm between you and debt.

CONTENTS

CONTENTS

INTRODUCTION

"One day you will tell your story of how you overcame what you went through, and it will be someone else's survival guide."

Casandra Brene Brown

American Research Professor, Author and Podcast Host

My mobile phone rang, with the caller ID clearly indicating who the caller was; the one person I couldn't run away from, even if I wanted to—my wife!

I sighed, took a few lungful of troubled breaths, and tried my hardest to keep a gentleman's composure. I was ill at ease, hoping the tone of my voice wouldn't give me away. What was going on in my head was more than a brainstorm—it was mental dystopia, the post-apocalyptic kind!

I opened my mouth hesitantly and quipped,

"Hello Babe."

The languor of my salutation was shot down by my wife's well-contained displeasure. Her words hit me hard from the other end of the line, like thunderbolts from the heavens.

"Chris, who are you?" asked my wife with unfathomable

disappointment in her voice.

I could tell she had been crying before she put that call through to me. She was seven months pregnant with our second child, and I had systematically (in hindsight, foolishly) kept her in the dark about my mountainous debt portfolio. With the excuse (undeniable fear) that I would never forgive myself if anything ever happened to her or the baby due to my actions and/or inactions.

Unfazed and undistracted by my empty machismo, she repeated her question like a lawyer doing a cross examination in the law court.

As a trained lawyer myself, I knew all too well to avoid her leading questions. I thought my legal skills would wriggle me out of this logjam, but her tenacity made it an uphill task. I was hopeless and shot a flare in the dark, hoping for an opening to scamper through and escape this dreaded position I had found myself in.

'What happened?' was the best reply my brain could come up with. To be honest, the words sheepishly rolled off my tongue, but the question was repeated a second time for emphasis, and now with renewed anger mixed with disgust, "Chris, who are you?"

At that point, the harsh reality finally dawned on me. I had inevitably put myself in an unenviable position where I was no longer recognizable to myself, my wife and, I am sure, to hundreds of others with whom I had built solid friendships over the years. It was at this point that I finally chose to swallow my pride and toe the path of surrender and redemption. I would later discover a creditor had called my wife and painted a horrid picture of what had been a well-kept secret up to that point. The creditor told my wife that she was married to a chronic and incorrigible debtor. He even questioned her sanity on why she was still married to me. He spewed more bile along with truckloads of unsolicited advice in a bid to recover an overdue debt.

The gentleman, a friend of two decades, would later on go to my office in my absence, and turn it upside down, just to make a point of his capacity to recover what was rightfully due to him, in a business transaction gone awry.

I admitted on that black day that I was wrong. I had, through my tainted vision and accumulated baggage of errors, mixed with faulty actions and inactions, found myself in a cesspool of debt and was drowning. I could hardly breathe with the stench of uncharitable opinions of me, the slime of abuses and curses, and the long gorings inflicted on my credibility, amongst others, that made it so difficult to climb out. It was official; I was scalp-deep in the morass of all-consuming debt. My world was darker than the chambers of Hades. I spent the next few months and years dealing with the legitimate salvos from incensed creditors while I tried to reset everything about my life as a husband, father, servant of God, and entrepreneur.

This book is probably one of the hardest books I would ever have to write because it is a byproduct of the lowest and most vulnerable moments of my pilgrimage on earth. It almost feels like an X-ray of my gut. It started as a painful undertaking until it gradually became cathartic for me. Which is why I believe it would be a blessing to many out there stuck in knotty debt.

I understand the economies of the nations in the twenty-first century are built on debt, and western finance gurus say debt is not necessarily a bad thing. As a Christian and victim of debt, which, in fact, was of extinction proportions, I would humbly submit that debt of any kind must be approached with caution. The Bible frowns upon reckless borrowing of any shade and size; we now have nations selling their future generations due to debt.

I have tried to present the reality I faced in a simple yet autobiographical form. I am a witness to the horrors of debt, with a debt profile of what was close to the equivalent of **$1,000,000**. One million dollars is a huge amount of money anywhere in the world! I was in deep trouble. So deep was the trouble that, for the first time in my life, contemplated suicide. But through the steps outlined in this book, I became a survivor by God's divine grace. And by the wisdom accessible only through His Spirit and word, which I had previously and stupidly ignored, I would go on to proffer practical steps that, when learned, were light to my feet in fleeing like a gazelle from the hand of the hunter in getting me to a place of financial freedom. In the words of Nelson Mandela, it has been a long walk to freedom!

Debt is a cruel monster. Just close your eyes and conjure the worst mental imagery your mind can conceive of what debt can look like. I assure you, even if painted by a medieval artist of repute, you still won't come close in painting this devious, unforgiving, ruthless creature on a canvas. It is a fact that it has destroyed the lives of millions and keeps a large percentage of today's modern world in its greasy grip of unremunerated servitude and non-negotiable stagnation.

The real proof of pudding is in the eating; this book therefore is my modest and honest attempt, with the help of the Holy Spirit, to help every reader see debt in its true Stygian form and colours. And not through the mentally glazed glasses of limited perspective, which is one of its tools of operation. Also, to debunk some myths surrounding this monster, I have tried to be as forthright as possible to help you take note of its insidious nature as it begins to swell like a cancerous growth in your financial space. I have also explained how to examine the risks to ensure you have a good rethink, identify clearly how people get into debt, and learn the strategies and actions to take to get out of debt quickly. Using my experience as reference, I have also identified and enumerated key decisions to make to avoid having repeated cycles of debt. Finally, and most importantly, how you can go on to recreate your life just like I did.

This is a real-life, practical book of hope. I have done my best to avoid technobabble and overspeak. I have the scars of debt, but that's how you truly learn, and you don't have to repeat my errors and those of others. I would rather point you in another direction toward freedom and abundance. This way, you won't have to witness firsthand these unpalatable horrors. After all, it is better to learn from the instructions and unpleasant experiences of others. This book is also a watchtower to those not in debt to steer the ships of their lives far from the hard rocks of debt island by avoiding the tempting, sonorous lilting of mystical sirens found in folklore that brought many seamen to their ruin.

Remember this: **almost anyone can find themselves in a debt spiral,** so don't hurt yourself any further. Now hold my hand and walk with me; I have been there and survived. You too can be debt-free!

Finally, and most importantly, my conclusion is that a departure from following laid down biblical principles concerning my finances was a sure recipe for my financial disaster. This is why you will find a handful of Bible quotes spread throughout this book. Biblical injunctions are meant to be followed to get you out of debt, and more importantly, stay debt-free. It is my sincere prayer that this book leads you back to the Scriptures to guide you (…thy word is truth"; John 17:17, KJV), through your earthly sojourn, where money plays a major role. It is your survival guide to getting out, but more importantly, staying out of debt.

The truths in Scripture carry with them a promise of God's power to help you overcome debt. Not just the truth, but the truth that you know; if you don't know the truth, you cannot walk in it (John 8:32).

PS: Throughout this book, I have tried to respectfully share stories and avoid using the names of people involved.

CHAPTER 1

WHAT IS DEBT?

"I have got some scars
but that's how you learn."

Song- Million Little Miracles
Old Church Basement
Elevation Worship & Maverick City Music

D ebt is a monster!

There you go. Think of horror movies or anything that makes your skin crawl with goose bumps. Catch my drift yet? Okay, so let's start by first considering some academic definitions of debt.

According to Wikipedia,

> *"Debt is an obligation that requires one party,
> the debtor, to pay money or any other agreed
> upon value to another party."*

Simply put, debt is something owed to another (for our discussion, we shall centre on money, but it could also be goods). Another apt description, regardless of how modern culture labels it, is that debt is a spirit; it is a ruling spirit whose sole aim is to push you to servitude. Debt is a carnivorous beast that feeds on your very best dreams.

In my case, debt was money borrowed by me from other parties to purchase what I couldn't readily afford at the time, used to service other debts, and used to fund business ventures that did not do well. Debt clearly is as old as man himself, but its existence through the annals of time doesn't justify its determination to enforce its undignified existence in the lives of men.

The vicissitudes of life, economies in a tailspin, rising costs of goods/ services, inflation, and over a thousand other reasons have a way of necessitating the justification for debt. But its often-neglected side effect or backlash is likened to a volcano filled with larva that erupts without a moment's notice, leaving in its aftermath tears, devastation, and sometimes death.

A firm realization must be established that regardless of the needs/wants that necessitate it, debt is simply a bondage that no man should be in. Little wonder even Jesus Christ in the Bible avoided debt, when he and Peter were approached by tax collectors (Matthew 17:24 – 27, KJV). I learnt the very hard way that debt is a poisoned chalice that seemed attractive at first but soon became extremely unpleasant in every conceivable way.

While there are descriptions of the various types of debt in our modern world, with organizations and countries knee-deep, we have often seen the dangers of debt and its multifarious boomerangs. Economists and financial analysts may argue on the need for a debt-run economy (this book is not written specifically to those organizations and countries, who may have justifiable parameters to engage debt options), but to you holding this book and how you run your personal life and business, and the danger of anchoring your existence on debt.

In my experience, it is evident that debt starts in the mind, and it is important to stress this point because all the physical actions you take start with your mind conceptualizing them. Your thoughts become feelings, and those feelings become actions. The debt I found myself in started in my mind, and in the words of my dear friend and debt coach, Titilope Ibilola, it stems from a scarcity mindset and a fear of the unknown. The same level of thinking and effort employed in getting into debt, I have since discovered, can be rechanneled into other activities that can lead you along the path of financial freedom, rather than being indebted to individuals and organizations.

In the face of pressing needs, most individuals find themselves befuddled, which makes them unable to think objectively, and debt is often the easiest option for them to get a quick fix like an addict would. Unbeknownst to them, debt, like a first-grade opioid, only gives them temporary reprieve and plunges them deeper into more financial mess; making them need more and more of it just to get by. What debt cannot solve; more debt would surely exacerbate it. This is true across most cultures in the world today. In life generally, quick fixes lead to quick nixes.

There is a monstrous industry that creates, packages, and wholesales debt. In my home country of Nigeria, for example, there has been a proliferation of loan apps in the past decade that has made borrowing online as dangerously ubiquitous as porn. More often than not, victims of this industry end up like sailors shipwrecked on an island unable to get off and are surrounded by the raging seas filled with creatures ready to make them fish food. The natural response of many is to take this as fate's sleight of hand. This ought not to be so. The whole idea of this book is to point out patterns to look out for, and to identify loopholes before they become too obvious and consume you totally. You can be masterfully enabled to learn from real-life tales on how to reclaim your freedom.

Is debt expressly referred to as a sin in scripture? No. But it is a weight. "Lay aside every weight and every sin," is what Hebrews 12:1 (NIV) says. Debt is a huge weight that slows down even the strongest, wisest and most determined of us all. Imagine having to run a 100 meters sprint race while your ankle is shackled with heavy weights. Despite your noble desire, be assured that nothing you are endowed with will suffice to win the race with the physical weights you are tied to. It's very hard to see a man make a success of his life, with debt looming over every action, and eavesdropping on every single conversation. It's time to cut off that weight, but first, let's examine a few common ways people get into debt.

HOW DO PEOPLE GET INTO DEBT?

Nothing sells a false fantasy better than debt. It is an Oscar-winning Hollywood production with the capacity to put up the best picture with you cast in the starring role without having an audition.

Almost all debts appear benign at the start, like a tumor that could be non-invasive and not cause any serious harm or trouble, but suddenly becomes cancerous, and the patient is staring at an almost certain, inevitable ruin, and a slow run to death. That's how dangerous debt really is. In some cases, it causes the real death of the individual who is at its mercy. So how does something that appears so harmless at the start turn around to make your past look like a hopeless dream; make your present feel like a nightmarish tale composed in the depths of hell; and finally, make your future look more senseless than a TV set tuned to dead channel?

How then do people get into debt? This list may not be by any means exhaustive, but a large percentage of readers will find a place of familiarity to their present or past situations embedded in one or more of the following:

1. Disobedience

Disobedience is often the rude and ill-mannered chauffeur that sits in the driver's seat of the debt vehicle. Disregard to God's instructions will lead to your driving in the direction of curses instead of blessings.

But it shall come to pass, that thou will not harken unto the voice of the Lord thy God, to observe to do all His commandments and His statutes which I command thee this day; that all these curses shall come upon thee, and overtake thee (Deuteronomy 28:15, KJV).

In verses 43 and 44 of the same chapter, it says,

"The stranger that is within thee shall get up above thee very high; and thou shall come down very low. He shall lend to thee, and thou shall not lend to him: he shall be the head, and thou shall be the tail".

Disobedience to the eternal truths contained in the Bible is thus a major reason people find themselves in debt. This is because they have strayed off the highway of wisdom, and have elected to take short cuts through dusty, forgotten, desolate pathways that are void of God's traffic warnings (mercy) and his law enforcement mechanism stationed for their financial security.

2. The Mind

"Do not conform to the pattern of this world,
but be transformed by the renewing of your mind.
Then you will be able to test and approve what God's
will is—his good, pleasing and perfect will."
- Romans 12:3, NIV

Debt is more than an amount of money owed; it is a way of thinking.

I often stared hard into the mirror, and never once did I feel like I was a hardened criminal or a heartless individual possessed by avarice. I have never wittingly gone to bed or woken up with the slightest intent to cause harm to another person. But having been embroiled in debt, there I was hurting and causing pain to people around me. I therefore came to this conclusion: debt doesn't necessarily make you a bad person, but it makes your decision-making very suspect.

I LOST ONE SUPERHUMAN ABILITY: the ability to control my mind, which influenced my decisions, and this clearly was the foundation stone of my debt edifice.

There is always going to be a conscious mental decision to either get into debt or not, and this is a fact. Every debt-related decision made was hardly induced but rather triggered by faulty thinking. It is important that

I stress that the battle of debt is won or lost in the grand coliseum of your mind. The physical expression or manifestation of the reality of a debt situation is often nothing more than a mirror reflection of a mental battle one has lost by agreeing to give up freedom and be a slave to debt. There are always two choices:

1. The hard choice of laying ego aside, being patient, being content, giving up unnecessary luxuries, living lean, working hard, and trusting God to open doors.

2. Throwing all caution to the wind and embracing the easy way out by means of debt.

The absence of positive and fortified mental warriors, will see many engage in a mental battle of wits that see them constantly on the losing side, pushing them further down the dark, lonely, and fearful highway of debt.

Many of us have been raised and conditioned environmentally to see debt as a normal way of life. We are carrying faulty paradigms, which are the escalators that aid the descent into the hell hole of debt, and they need to be dislodged. Dr. Caroline Leaf, in her book, Switch on Your Brain, puts it succinctly:

*"As we think, we change the physical
nature of our brain. As we consciously direct*

*our thinking, we can wire our thinking and
replace it with healthy thoughts."*

In Romans 12:13, we can clearly identify a major problem: that many of us have conformed to the pattern of this world, with our approach towards the acceptable norm of living day by day in debt, and this is not the will of the creator. Every time we go against His ordained will, the result is always one of pain and disaster. The constant renewal of the mind is the only fortified barrier that can resist the onslaught of pressures and temptations that cause our descent into pain. Another faulty mindset paradigm that leads to debt is the scarcity mindset stated earlier, a state that keeps you in perpetual desperation, while ignoring the reality that the world is filled with so much abundance, of which you can partake while leaving much more for others to enjoy. This mindset must be aborted without delay.

In life, you don't choose consequences; you make choices, and those choices will unilaterally create the consequences. Therefore, don't for a second doubt the efficacy of the law of cause and effect, especially when it comes to debt. The starting point of how people get into debt is their inability to be masters of their minds.

3. Pride/Ego

*"Pride leads to disgrace,
but with humility comes wisdom."*
- *Proverbs 11:2, NIV*

The word ego points at an exaggerated sense of self-importance, which results in excessive preoccupation of self. My wife, Oduola, is one woman blessed with senses that I sometimes refer to as above-human capacity. She has her Super Woman moments, where her extrahuman senses are able to sniff trouble a mile away. Those who lack this sixth-sense ability will almost certainly find themselves in debt, just like I did from overthinking my capabilities, which led to an inflated ego. I ignored the gifts and capacities of those positioned around me who would have signaled that I was skating on thin ice.

This lack of humility caused me dearly and greatly. The absence of vulnerability towards my wife when it came to money issues led me to financial ruin and eventually behind the iron bars of the prison of debt. It is also one of the leading reasons people remain in debt after getting into debt. Their pride/ego is constantly at play.

I grew up always occupying leadership positions in schools, social settings, and community affairs. At some point, I felt like a special plant whose tendrils were destined to touch and absorb the best largesse of the high heavens. It was a case of me having confidence in my imagined competence. I felt I was the alpha male, answerable to no one but myself. This blindside led me drowsily to the rocks, and before I knew it, it was lights out!

I was blessed and given a super hero wife, yet I ignored her super abilities that would have helped me to be more disciplined with money. Had I subscribed to the loving, preclusive services of her senses to avoid certain individuals and let go of a number of business opportunities, I probably would have been spared. But again, my pride/ego blindfolded me to all of this with the belief that my vulnerability would be equal to my weakness.

For many years, my inability to admit the need for assistance in managing money caused ballooned debts in my life. Pride will make you spend unnecessary dollars when you should be seeking a bargain. Pride will keep you from asking for help when the ground starts giving way. Pride will reinforce the faulty paradigms that you can do it all by yourself. Pride will strengthen the negative resolve that no one needs to know you are drowning. Pride and ego are the rungs on the shaft that descend straight into the flesh-grinding, murky belly of the beast called debt.

4. Ostrich Mentality

"Don't run from trouble. Take it full-face.
The "worst" is never the worst."
- Lamentations 3:30, Msg

While the myth of ostriches burying their heads in the sand when scared or threatened is widespread, the truth is they do dig holes to bury their heads in the sand several times a day. They however, bury their heads to turn their eggs. It is still exactly what many of us do, and that gets us into debt.

We carry on like it's business as usual, with the expectation that the winds of life will just come along and blow away all of our financial problems without us taking any form of responsibility. It is a fact that ignoring a glaring problem has never been the answer or solution especially when it comes to debt. Millions are in debt and remain in debt today due to this singular, heartfelt, wishful desire of waking up to a utopian outcome like a mythical Disney character and all its happily ever after. If you ever want to avoid getting into debt, you must face your realities as they are and be productive in your thinking. Many individuals stack their monthly bills as they arrive in the post with no intention of taking action. Many others receive letters in the post from bankers or bailiffs without taking the necessary action to open a negotiation. They would rather just "hope" that, somehow, their bills and unresolved financial issues would vaporize into thin air like solid air fresheners. While hope is a good thing in all things living, this brand of hope is dysfunctional at best and only gets you into deeper debt when you choose to live alone in your fool's paradise. Hope is not a strategy to becoming financially free.

5. Societal/Cultural Influences

"Those who love money will never have enough. How meaningless to think that wealth brings true happiness."
- Ecclesiastes 5:10, NIV

If you come from certain regions of the world, like Africa, where I am from, you may quickly identify this Bible verse as being explicit with the truth on the reason why people are in debt and, unfortunately, without transformation and light, may die in debt. Society places a demand on all of us, whether it's on our time or freedom, but especially on our finances.

In Africa, where the concept of family and community living is far-reaching, it appears almost impossible not to be drawn into that maze of demands from someone or something that does not participate in or directly benefit your life. It's referred to as Black Tax, money made especially by professionals and those with higher income given to parents, siblings, or other family members, often out of obligation or a deeply ingrained sense of responsibility.

There just always seems to be a reason to be paying or spending for something that does not even tangentially align with your destiny. In most cases, whether or not you can afford it is immaterial. From weddings, to funerals, to someone's coronation, and all sorts of money-grubbing schemes, you are literally required to cough out monies you do not have to spare. Whole industries have been built around frivolities. It is fashionable for someone to feed a whole community for days because they want to bury a loved one. You are a villain if you do not splurge. There is a psychological pull and push—stress and strain for you to live up to these toxic cultural expectations whether you can afford it or not.

The term, keeping up with the Joneses, is another popular reference to our desire to match up to society or cultural influences, even at the detriment of our financial security and future. We try to emulate or not be outdone by one's neighbors. Therefore, when analyzed, we often go into debt because of envy. Many are in debt due to caring way too much about what people think, feel, or say. They instead prefer to put themselves in the firing range for target practice by creditors. It would shock you if you do a mental recall of where the chunk of your spending went. The harsh results will probably reveal that a major slice of your resources in the financial pie chart went directly or indirectly into expenditures that have no bearing to your growth/progression. Neither should they have representation in your budgets (if you have one) just to keep up with appearances.

The race for bigger, better, and newer of everything is the greatest tragedy to befall our present generation. From the newest devices to the fastest cars, to the poshest homes (and while I may stress these things on their own are not wrong, their acquisition at the expense of your financial freedom can lead to debt and adoption by its mother poverty) which further tightens the shackles of debt, therefore making it one of the leading causes of financial meltdown. Societal influences make us steal from our future earning potential so that we can get an instant gratification that comes from maintaining meaningless, hollow status symbols that have no real value to our future.

6. Interest

> *"we nothing to anyone—except*
> *for your obligation to love one another."*
> *- Romans 13:8, NIV*

The Talmud, which is the ancient Jewish text for Jewish laws, quotes an ancient rabbi as saying:

*"It is better to sell your
daughter into slavery than to
borrow money on interest."*

If there was one gremlin that called the shots in my personal debt battle, it was the gladiator called interest. I struggled more with interest payments from credit cards, appliance purchases, and personal and business loans because they all had in common one feature: a singular duty or function, which is to stand by the iron bars and, despite my best efforts, keep me trapped in the prison of debt. Our world, like I have earlier indicated, is seemingly awash with credit for almost everything and anything; even corporate organizations that were the only nemesis or villains seem to have passed on this virus to individuals who want in on the action.

I engaged foolishly and naively in financial dealings with a kindergarten mindset of outrunning interests. While this is not an impossibility for some, the strong vines of interest always seemed to catch up with me and suck up cash that could have been better utilized for other investment purposes to get me out of debt. The minute you or the business you run is unable to make those interest payments, Armageddon is immediately invited to your doorstep. Interests are more inflammable than the most inflammable gas on the planet, chlorine trifluoride, which can burn through concrete and gravel, and would burn down your finances if you let them!

Remember those Hollywood flicks where mobsters tried to get rid of their real or perceived enemies and would tie the legs of some poor unfortunate person to concrete and allow them to be thrown into a body of water? That concrete weight you see is interest; there is only one way to go when you are tied to it, and that is down. No matter how much you struggle—in fact, the more you struggle, the faster you are headed down to the seabed of despair.

I remember reading a very interesting and life-changing story from the scriptures about a man called Nehemiah who was the cupbearer to King Artaxerxes, the then global ruler of his age. Nehemiah had undeniably found favour with God and man; with the permission of the great king, he returned back to the destroyed city of Jerusalem to rebuild first its walls and then its gates. But a very interesting discourse got my attention in Nehemiah 5 (NIV). It had come to his attention how interests were ruining people and making them poor, and in verse 10 of the same chapter, he remarked:

"I and my brothers and my men
are also lending the people money and grain.
But let us stop Charging Interest!"

The lesson for me was all too glaring: you can never escape from poverty or debt when you have the yoke of interest stretching your spine beyond breaking point. Its noose is usually so tight that it brings an inevitable end—financial strangulation. The Jews who complained to Nehemiah were mortgaging their fields, vineyards, and homes, and had to borrow money to even pay tax. They had their children enslaved and Nehemiah said when he heard their outcry and "these charges, I was very angry."

If you never want to be caught up in a web of debt, avoid anything with a tag of interest. Though appealing and soothing to begin, it usually masks itself until it is the right time to strike. It is a never-ending rabbit hole to travel down into. The days leading up to interest payments run faster than Olympians, and it is a fact that most creditors tend to profit more when you default with penalties. So, it is never a win-win scenario; interest is a pointer to debt, and no tide is more overwhelming to your life's boat than that of interests.

7. Inability to Delay Gratification

"But let patience have its perfect work, that you may be perfect and complete, lacking nothing."
- James 1:4, KJV

Debt is a procrastinator's way of spending money; you are borrowing against your future self for immediate gratification. The absence of patience cost me so much during my trials of debt.

Delayed gratification is one of the hallmarks of financially free individuals, and it simply means the discipline to give up something now to obtain a better reward in the future. But it is easier to define than to execute, and I found out the very hard way.

Delayed gratification demands a great deal of discipline, self-mastery, and willpower—qualities I was deficient in, and I can probably speak for quite a number of individuals in today's modern world.

Famous debt coach, Dave Ramsey, defines it in one single word, "immaturity." So clearly, we may be physically and psychologically mature, psychologically mature but many are financially immature and like all immature individuals, there is a price to pay for this shortcoming. Which in most instances is debt. Adults devise plans and follow through on them; children do what feels good. The financial decisions (every decision actually) we make today are pointers to the results in our lives waiting for us tomorrow.

Many of you are eating away tomorrow's opportunities; in my case, the inability to delay gratification saw me mostly eating both the seed and bread of my income. According to 2 Corinthians 9:10, *"Now he who supplies seed to the sower and bread for food..."* the clear distinction is that a man who refuses to delay gratification will not sow and eat most or all.

We live in a microwave generation that demands everything to be ready at the snap of their fingers. Name it: from your instant noodles, quick coffee, news & information, e.t.c., and we look with disdain at any doctrine or philosophy that seeks to slow down the speed of our consumerism. It takes hard work, sacrifice, discipline, and diligence to delay what is right in front of you. I must again admit that life happens, and with the daily barrage of temptations all our senses are exposed to, with the relentless assaults, we are almost unable to mentally calculate and critically think through what really matters. We are constantly made to choose between spending now and enjoying some gratification or saving/ investing now and enjoying a bigger fulfillment later. Undelayed gratification is thus listed by many leading financial experts as one of the major reasons behind debt accumulation. That is why you have got to trade what you want right now for what you truly need later, and in Dave Ramsey's words, "Don't make silly money decisions just because you couldn't tell yourself 'no' in the moment." I made those silly money decisions with my inability to say no, and I paid the hefty price.

8. Surety

*"Don't agree to guarantee another person's debt
or put up security for someone else. If you can't pay it,
even your bed will be snatched from under you."*
- Proverbs 22:26–27, NIV

It may actually shock you to know that standing as a surety, is a leading cause of how people find themselves in debt and often times one of the most painful, because you probably played no part in spending or benefiting directly and you pay the price like you did.

The book of Proverbs 6:1-3 (NIV), describes this in detail:

*"My son, if you have put up security
for your neighbor, if you have been trapped
by what you said, ensnared by the words of
your mouth. So do this, my son, to free yourself,
since you have fallen into your neighbor's hands:
Go-to the point of exhaustion-and give
your neighbor no rest!"*

Clearly, it's stupid to guarantee someone else's loan; most of the time, standing as surety is a sure way to debt. While I am aware that many times it is done from a place of love and a desire to help those we care about who may be in need, it is suicidal to be responsible for actions you can't undertake or guarantee their outcome.

It is why Proverbs 17:18, AMP, describes such a man as lacking common sense who gives a pledge, and becomes guarantor (for the debt of another) in the presence of his neighbor.

9. Life's Curve Balls

"I've learned over and over that life
happens on its own terms, not mine."
- Kate Walsh

In Ecclesiastes 3:1, King Solomon wrote, "There is ...*There is an appointed time for everything. And a time for every event under heaven...*"

This is one factor that may be well beyond us; I call them the gray areas, which we can't explain. In legal parlance, we have a similar scenario that can help me explain better; it is called force majeure, and in everyday language, it is called an act of God. This may mean a sudden loss of job, unfavorable government policies, an unfortunate accident, a heart-wrenching divorce, devastating health issues, painful death, and even an unprecedented global pandemic like the COVID-19, e.t.c. The list is seemingly unfolding, and unending, but any of these may accelerate you towards the path of debt. Our reality is that there is a time for every event under heaven.

"Moreover, no one knows when their hour will come: As fish are caught in a cruel net, or birds are taken in a snare, so people are trapped by evil times that fall unexpectedly upon them." (Ecclesiastes 21:9, NIV)

One minute everything seems to be working according to the game plan, the next minute you are forced to downsize on everything you have become accustomed to. And you have a mountain of debt that seems to have appeared from nowhere, painfully dwarfing all your possibilities. Your income becomes no more than vapor, which is intangible and unable to be utilized. Though there are mitigation steps against such curve balls that life throws at each and every one of us, in different shapes, sizes, and impacts, life's events can surely lead you to debt. They often blindside you especially when you are unprepared for such events, and your inability to respond appropriately often leads us to emotional decisions that spell disaster in the long run.

10. Insufficient Income

"The thoughts of the diligent tend
only to plenteousness, but of everyone
who is hasty only to want."
- Proverbs 21:5, KJV

Higher outgoings/lower income are clearly the perfect recipe for a debt dish. Such dishes are served cold and are often hard and difficult to swallow and digest. Life is clearly unforgiving, as our existence in a modern world full of freak shows is clearly skewed against millions who run a rat race trying to keep up with their bills.

The reason many are in debt is because the expected outgoings clearly tilt the scales against the very low incomes coming in. Therefore, it's a never-ending game of catch, that age old children's game that many adults never get out of and keep playing to their graves. The very moment what you earn or generate is unable to handle your bills, you will have debt on your front porch like a dedicated salesman demanding an audience. There are three possible co-travelers with insufficient income: lying, stealing, and more significantly, for this discourse, debt.

11. Greed and Lack of Self-control

"And he said to them, take care
and be on your guard against all covetousness
for one's life does not consist in the
abundance of his possessions."
– Luke 12:15, NIV

Yes, greed!

The word sounds very condescending, almost like an annoying tag you forgot to take off on that newly purchased shirt, dress, or new pair of shoes. But greed is one of the leading cause of debt. Your inability to imbibe the necessary discipline and self-control over different areas of your life all accumulates to debt.

Many of us struggle with greed, and it's no joke. Many individuals desire everything they gaze on as a matter of right, and when the inability to possess what the eyes lust after occurs, the apparent, obvious resultant effect is DEBT. If you want to know why millions are drowning in the waters of debt, it is, in many cases, caused by the alluring services of Mr. Greed.

12. Lack of Financial Education

"A wise man will hear, and will increase learning: and a man of understanding shall attain unto wise counsels:
- Proverbs 1:5, KJV

The very lack of basic financial education is a forerunner of debt. Many individuals do not invest, save, or care about the need to be empowered with relevant knowledge to keep them safe from debt. They are often the ones guided by ego, scoffing at those who invest resources and time, learning and absorbing knowledge on being financially free and independent. Robert Kiyosaki, the famous author of the hugely successful financial roadmap "Rich Dad, Poor Dad," would identify that you can be highly educated, experienced and still be financially illiterate which will lead you to debt.

13. Lack of Emotional Intelligence

"Guard your heart above all else,
for it determines the course of your life."
- Proverbs 4:23, NIV

Emotional Intelligence (EI) is simply the cognitive ability to identify, process, and manage emotions. Nothing most likely stirs our emotional pot like money does. Whether it is making or spending it. Money is undeniably intricately tied to emotions. There are findings that there are emotion-laden connotations related to the notion of money. My attitude about money and disbursing it as I deemed fit were determined by my ability to manage emotion-related issues. Therefore, my basic lack of understanding of my emotions, perceptions, triggers, and blind spots, were all incompetences that teleguided me to a place of debt.

I remember once dating a young lady who clearly

understood the power of manipulation and a man's ego. She would make financial demands of me, and for whatever reasons, would anchor it firmly on my inability to provide for someone who I claimed to love. Unfortunately, she cared little about how I was going to make that money (she was a missile dodged). I would have my emotions troubled, tossed like clothes in a washing machine, all in a bid to prove myself to be a man. Many, regardless of gender, have found themselves in emotional blackmail situations, leading to more financial difficulties.

Your beliefs, when it comes to your money, must be X-rayed to ensure that you are not reinforcing patterns that guarantee debt. We all have diverse backgrounds governed by culture, mindsets, and our programming, which are often conditioned by our environment, upbringing and defining emotional experiences are what guide some of our individual approaches toward our finances. Unfortunately, millions get into debt due to the faulty nature of their programming. This is a silent and often ignored but salient factor behind debt.

CHAPTER 3

WHAT ARE THE RISKS OF DEBT?

---

*"For they sow the wind
and reap the whirlwind."*

Hosea 8:7, NIV

I n Africa, there is a particular rodent mostly found in the villages. What makes this rodent different from its city cousins is a unique trait it possesses: while you are asleep at night, it has this uncanny mischievous ability of chewing away at its victim's body parts—usually the fingers, toes, and earlobes. Its flesh-chewing is usually done with the most premium stealth and insidious tact. Often, when the victim feels a level of discomfort, the rat is known to blow cool, soothing air on the wound, so that the victim is not too discomforted to awaken. By the time the victim manages to finally awaken, they have already parted ways with some substantial chunks of their flesh. That's a graphic description of debt.

I was relatively well-respected to a very high degree in the public eye with my public speaking engagements, online mentoring, e.t.c., during my wilderness experience of indebtedness. Debt was clearly ready to make me pay the ultimate price of giving up all I had worked for. My embedded sociable demeanor hardwires me to make friends easily, and I lost the respect of a good number of friends. I still received speaking invitations, many of which I felt like declining because I felt like a fraud, carrying a load larger than that of John Bunyan's pilgrim classic Pilgrim's Progress. The late American Evangelist Oral Roberts, in his book, When You See the Invisible You Can Do the Impossible, would help me capture the thoughts of someone in the spotlight facing challenges and sums it all up thus:

"When you are in the limelight
as long as I have been, your losses and
defeats are easier seen by others,
increasing the pressure on your spirit.
Of course, whether you are exposed to large
segments of the public or not, any loss or
defeat hurts your heart."

What are the risks you run into when you find yourself in debt?

It will hurt. Debt hurts badly; it really hurts badly.

There is hardly a more devastating scenario that can confront a mortal man like debt. I liken it to a volcanic eruption, which usually occurs when enough magma builds up in the magma chamber of a huge rock formation, forces its way up to the surface, and explodes, often causing volcanic eruptions. That is the process of debt—slowly building and climaxing in a tumult first in the soul—and you are overflowing on the surface with hot lava, destroying everything in its path. The debtor is often unable to elude this hot destructive lava, or if that is too hot for you to process, let me cool it down with some ice.

Imagine skiing on the beautiful Swiss Alps in Zermatt or St. Moritz, two popular locations for skiers, and there is a tremor or a natural disturbance forcing the mountains to awaken from their deep slumber to shake off hundreds of feet of snow down on you while yawning. No matter the safety gear you possess or the speed you conjure to escape such an avalanche, you are most likely unable to escape the most probable outcome: death!

If many understood the risks of debt and made better decisions on the subject of finance, I strongly believe that the mental and physical bombardments many are under would have been avoided because all final decisions have consequences, some of which you may be forced to live with, like Jacob had to with a limp acquired from his angelic battle. I still remember occasions when my spouse attended events and was forced to sit on the same table with previous or then present creditors, some of whom were my former school mates and contemporaries. She would express her pain from such inevitable encounters on her return, and all I was able to offer were sincere apologies. Debt hurts.

I personally discovered that debt enables you to

contemplate realities you naturally never thought possible; it is a rude door opener. For many, they turn to hard drugs, alcohol, etc. Some just abscond and give up on the lives they have built, while others take the ultimate and unfortunate decision of playing their last card with life by committing suicide. Therefore, this and other following risks are to serve as a yellow card, a warning before disaster to anyone attempting to tread the ignoble path of debt. It will help to be a deterrent while also preparing the mind of someone who is already neck-deep in debt, not to throw in the towel but to toughen the mind and body for what may come their way.

1. Debt Affects Your Income and Limits Your Ability to Provide

*"Anyone who does not provide
for their relatives, and especially for
their own household, has denied the faith
and is worse than an unbeliever."*
- 1 Timothy 5:8, NIV

Debt will greatly mangle your income streams like nothing else can. Every dime you muster or come up with goes into servicing it. This inadvertently handicaps your ability to survive, save for your future, and grow exponentially financially. This was a huge struggle, I must confess.

The major challenge that confronted me was my inability to provide where I had previously done. This did not only shatter my pride as a man; it also shook my marriage to its foundation. My immediate environment felt like quicksand. The centre hardly held as the turbulence increased with each passing day. I can't count the number of arguments with Oduola when the financial pressure became unbearable. There were many things to be taken care of: school fees, feeding, household bills, just name it. Debt reduced my ability to give my family the best of what they deserved. You must understand the older you become, the more you are responsible to provide skyrockets. I had a wife, a child, and an infant to take care of, but no matter how much love I had for them, I just couldn't live up to my responsibilities.

I have heard tales of many who ended their lives unable to leave a good inheritance for their family. This is another reality to be confronted, a fearful dream that debt will put on autoplay. If you don't want to witness a situation of seeing your family grow hungry, service providers hounding you over unpaid services, and government taxes piling up, you must understand that a major risk of debt is that it affects your income significantly, thus limiting your ability to provide, which is a divine duty given by God.

2. Time

*"To everything there is a season, and a time
to every purpose under the heaven."*
- Ecclesiastes 3:1, KJV

Nothing robs you of time like debt; you must first remember that the unit of destiny is time. I liken the measurement of time to the units in my home's electricity meter. The electricity, measured in kWh (The Kilowatt-hour), once exhausted means no electricity supply to my home.

God, in His infallible wisdom, recognizing the unique importance and potency of his creation 'time', knows that there are many things, such as debt lurking in the dark to distract us from things that truly matter. The American pastor and author Rick Warren described it this way, "Time is your most precious gift, because you have only a set amount of it."

One of the greatest risks you run with debt is that your allocation of time on the earth realm is effectively stolen from you. Why is the understanding of this point crucial? You might ask. Time is the currency of existence and the most valuable asset your destiny holds, not your houses, cars, or other material possessions. Debt creeps up and ensures that rather than being the master of your time to be a person of value and worshipping your creator through your actions, you do nothing but waste it, invariably making you its slave. You are unable to muster enough strength and courage to effectively manage and distribute your time as you deem fit; instead, you have debt through its human agents (creditors), calling the shots on how you spend something crafted by heavenly hands.

The long hours you spend pleading your case, reflecting on the what ifs, sleepless hours, the long phone calls, etc. all eat up the time that should be utilized in improving yourself and becoming valuable to your world. What debt does is that it converts you to live for others in a negative way that wasn't originally intended to be. This anomaly creates deep resentment for yourself and others—a risk I can assure you from experience is not one worth exploring.

3. Your Peace and Rest

"Now may the Lord of peace Himself give
you peace at all times and in every way..."
- 2 Thessalonians 3:16

It's no cliché that human beings tend to value things more when they lose them. We tend to underestimate the power of peace and rest to our overall well-being, whether physically or spiritually. The tranquility and freedom from the stress of other people or things are worth more than all the money circulating through the arteries of the global economy or marketplace.

There were days I sought peace and was willing to pay any price. God instituted man to rest after work, something He exemplified Himself after creation, and what debt does is eliminate, or better still, obliterate the ability to rest, replacing it with fiery anxiety and multiplying worries.

My waking moments were literally invested in drilling a hole of reprieve through the massive rock of debt in front of me. The after-tremors of holding that heavy rock drill machinery is occasionally felt. I remember without much joy how my mind would contemplate and explore any/every work option to augment my shortfalls. I would sometimes be forced to underprice my services and value to clients, occasionally to the chagrin of my team and spouse. You must understand that debt is leprous-hearted; it is much colder than a thousand-year-old fossil buried in Antarctica. With every phone call from creditors, debt collectors, concerned relatives, perceived friends, email from my bank or credit unions, and every WhatsApp message, I would simply lose a little more of the fragile sanity that I had until I started becoming numb; borderline psychotic.

In fact, for most people in debt, the Truecaller app almost

becomes the best technological creation of the twenty-first century because it furnishes them with the ability to screen calls and ascertain identities to dodge creditors (not something I encourage). But in culmination, even if you could evade everyone, there is a significant loss of peace that is almost as much a part of you as your own breath. Many in debt are unable to have a good night's rest. This is what drives some of them to alcoholism, hard drugs, and anything at all that can help them numb the pain from harassment, albeit temporarily.

The Bible says,

> *For the despondent,*
> *every day brings trouble..."*
> *(Proverbs 15:1, NLT)*

With uncertainty plaguing their minds about what a new day would present, debtors are simply deficient of peace. Do you seek to lead a peaceful life? Avoid debt. Period!

I belong to a few online debt groups, and the cries for help, desperation, suicide considerations, and the whole tragic stretch all add up to a colossal loss of peace. My sister would, in retrospect, occasionally comment on how, in the heat of my debt journey, there was no longer a clear demarcation between when it was day or night. In debt, it seemed it was always day because there was hardly any rest. The uncertainty robbed me and all who cared of appetite, focus, and peace. I would sit up all night while the world rested, unable to enjoy what should be natural and free—peace! At a point, I resorted to drugs to catch a good nap, but no matter how sweet the slumber was, by my bedside was the debt monster, which always latched back on to continue its job of torture, like a diligent worker clocking in for his shift.

Anyone who has experienced debt will tell you how it is normal to be held hostage, or better still captive, and systematically stripped of one's dignity.
Those are days I never want to replay, and there is a huge risk you stand to experience and witness if you choose debt.

4. Loss of Freedom

"I will walk in freedom, for I have devoted
myself to your commandments."
- Psalm 119:45, NIV

I clearly missed the Sunday school class where this Bible verse was taught. Otherwise, I would have recognized that not seeking and following the precepts of wisdom set out concerning money and debt would mean imprisonment, the direct opposite of liberty or freedom. Nothing robs you of the inherent God-given freedom you should naturally enjoy like debt does. It places you in captivity, a self-imposed prison, where you become very limited in your expression of where to go and who to see because of the fear of running into your creditors and the ensuing shame.

I vividly remember when I was hesitant to even go outside for a walk, or visit certain places. I couldn't even comment on WhatsApp groups, go to a familiar restaurant, or attend a party or public gathering. Those were days of real torture for myself and my loved ones. Man was created by the almighty to be free and not to be imprisoned; it is why solitary confinement is the apex of mental punishment that can be visited on an incarcerated individual. There is something about the loss of freedom and its effect on the human psyche, and very few things have the ability to have such a devastating effect on an individual like debt. I received invitations from law enforcement agencies, and in the part of the world I am from, such invites portend nothing but gloom and doom spawning drama that the pages of this book cannot sufficiently capture. Little wonder the psalmist said,

"When hard pressed, I cried to the Lord;
He brought me into a spacious place."
(Psalms 118:5, NIV)

One of the biggest risks is allowing debt to enforce its freedom-destroying mandate on you which keeps you hard pressed in a restricted space. This is definitely like being stretched beyond your breaking point. You must seek to resist this by paying the price of staying in your spacious place of freedom by avoiding debt altogether.

5. Addiction

"It teaches us to say 'no' to ungodliness
and worldly passions, and to live self-controlled,
upright and godly lives in this present age."
- Titus 2:12, NIV

Debt is like any other addiction, only in its case it stays in the corner like a sly feline—it has the compelling ability to keep its victim perennially hooked and fixated on it. With lethal capability, like that of a nuclear weapon, it can decimate anything and anyone it comes into contact with; great men have been brought down from horseback to walk on bare feet. In this case, like most addictions, its focus would be to destroy the body and mind of a man, just like gambling or even alcoholism.

A major risk you will encounter is how easy, tempting, and alluring it is to get into it. Like in my case, in the early days, the ride seemed smooth until it was not. I discovered that when debt became an addiction, it was readily the first thing that came to mind whenever I was in a financial rut. And because I allowed it, it festered and morphed into a beast that nearly swallowed me whole, if not for God's mercy. So, I began to experiment with taking on more debts to offset debts—like trying to quench a raging fire with more fuel or an inflammable liquid.

Ask any addict, and you will be confronted with the reality that in that exact moment that the thick blanket of addiction clouds your mind, it makes it nearly impossible to consider any other option that can lead you to the light of freedom. Debt presents itself as the only way. Do not be hoodwinked into that timeless, faulty mindset that you are confronted with only one option at any given point in time. Give it more thought, and if you can afford a little more time, you will be surprised at the plethora of options that were initially hidden beneath the surface. When confronted with tough times, this is a major mental paradigm shift, a mental deliverance.

Addictions, as you may well be aware, are like wet concrete—very easy to form and extremely difficult to break when dry. This is even truer when the pathways are already established in your mind. Therefore, it is a major risk to allow debt of any shade, form, or size into your life. It hardly ever wants to be a casual acquaintance but instead seeks to be a life-long partner, the one that you must never be tied to in unholy matrimony.

6. Bondage to People/Systems

*"No one can serve two masters, for either he will
hate the one and love the other, or he will be devoted
to the one and despise the other..."*
- Matthew 6:24, NIV

The Collins Dictionary defines bondage as the condition of being someone's property and having to work for them.

Debt is one slave master whose chains guarantee bondage to not just people's pockets. Stay with me to expatiate. When examining the situation where a man faces a debt debacle quite deeply, you will find out, that such an individual will also run the risk of being servile to systems and processes because of debt. You must fight with every fiber of your being to avoid anyone or thing owns you.

I ran through this unfortunate path, which led me to be bound, whether I recognized it at the moment or not. I was unequally yoked to my creditors; to their systems and structure, they could go on to effectively control what I could or couldn't do, where I could or couldn't go; whether I could post on social media or not etc. Debt is like a sticky spider web, almost invisible to the less observant eyes, until you find yourself wrapped up in it like an Egyptian mummy. A major risk you stand to suffer is being the property of people and the systems and processes they control.

7. Self-esteem

"And God saw everything he had made,
and behold it was very good."
- Genesis 1:31

"What have I done to you to deserve this level of fraud? Chris I won't curse you but will leave you in God's hand now that your intention has been so clear to me and after hearing about your records as a serial scammer."

The caustic words above once came in as a text message, and trust me, this was one of the nicest of the entire collection of poison pen texts I received from friends and business partners who were frankly frustrated with my inability to pay them what I owed them.

Nothing blasts your self-esteem to smithereens like debt. There were days that dysania got a full hold of me—when I wished I could just sleep on forever in my bed, totally cut off from the extant realities of my pain and struggles. I felt defeated and without any ounce of energy to get up and face the world.

Debt will attack your self-esteem like nothing else, and

the absence of a healthy self-esteem will suck out energy from you, even from the most stoical and strong-willed people.

You want to be able to face life, give it your best shot, and then avoid debt like a dreaded epidemic. The term social distancing is now part of our global lexicon, all thanks to the COVID-19 virus. It means giving the next person the most possible distance to avoid any form of infection. In the same vein, there must be social distancing between you and any form of debt.

You run the risk of living a very defeated and frustrated life in the absence of positive self-esteem. And nothing will ram into this, like calls from those trying to recover their monies, letters of demand, and emails of threats from lawyers, or even harassment from law enforcement agencies. Your character, like a bull's eye, will be placed in front of a firing squad once you take on the cloak of debt. It is the fastest way to lose respect in the eyes of others. Usually pictures from the past may elicit different emotions for me; those emotions were filled with nothing but regrets. I hated my old school pictures, old birthday parties; I had made a mess of it all. That's the risk of debt. It is a horrible, ripping sensation that never stops tearing and eating away at your homes and dreams.

8. Physical Harm/Threats

*"The rich rules over the poor,
and the borrower is slave to the lender."*
- Proverbs 22:7

Trust me when I say this: when it comes to debt, there are many scenarios but no rules; many moving parts but no coordination. More often than not, it is purely wild, like the Serengeti. Debt will introduce the wrong people into your life, tie you up in a knot of relationships that are one-sided, and only benefit the other party.

In one instance, I had a creditor (who also happened to be a friend of many decades) who, under the stress accrued of recovering a business loan from me, took the rash step of visiting my office and thrashing it. He was most livid, and not even the pleas of my pregnant wife could calm him down. The individual was hell-bent on taking his pound of flesh while yelling concentrated profanities into the office space. He at a point threatened to return to burn down my office. After he had satisfactorily established my absence, he went on to verbally assault clients of my wife, who at the time was sharing the same office space with me. This, of course, was another bolt of abuse I had to endure for the sake of debt. The very day this happened, it reinforced the realization that indeed, debt might have inspired the title of Tom Clancy's 1989 novel, A Clear and Present Danger.

Debt will have you scared of the shadow of a magnified mouse. The notification of a phone call with no caller ID will inject tons of paranoia into your mind. The threat to your very life and to your properties is REAL. Unfortunately, life is no Hollywood script; thus, such actions taken by creditors carry far-reaching repercussions some of which many individuals never recover from, even after the debts are paid. You don't deserve to look over your shoulders for the rest of your life, and you shouldn't run the risk of physical harm when you expose yourself to debt.

9. Reputation

"A good reputation is more
valuable than costly perfume."
Ecclesiastes 7:1, NIV

Debt will leave your reputation in tatters, it left mine in such a pitiable state. Reputational damage is almost a certain byproduct that accompanies an unfulfilled financial obligation to a third party whether it is an individual or organization. Once you accept debt, you run the risk of damaging a reputation that could have taken several years to build with unrecoverable sweat and huge sacrifice.

Again, I implore you to take it from someone who has been there, with thick, ugly scars to show. I remember once pitching a business idea to a prospective investor, who, despite the grandiose potential of the amazing financial returns, politely declined due to what someone had whispered in his ears. Clearly, he felt I was a reputational risk, which I probably was in light of my poor financial standing. Oh, how much it hurt to imagine that someone viewed me in such an unfavorable light. I moved around with the fear of what the other person perceived of me; this feeling permeated every cell in my body. On several occasions, I imagined myself carrying an offense board in a mug shot, which would be the final nail to my reputation. My financial existence was almost rootless, something no sane investor would want to be associated with, directly or indirectly.

In today's world, which is filled with slews of lending services where borrowing is made easy, you don't want to have financial institutions or debt agencies sink their fangs into you. It almost always does not end well.

In Nigeria, for instance, banks take the unconventional route of shaming debtors by taking out paid advertorials in major newspapers on a weekly basis. This is usually a last-ditch attempt at loan recovery, and it is done by displaying the names and images of individuals in the public domain, hopefully to shame them into paying. Any money owed and mounting interest, leaves reputations in tatters.

As I have already said, in recent times, online lending has been on the increase, with sums borrowed without any collateral (but ridiculous interest to follow) thus, attracting individuals who normally would have been excluded from considerations for loans from traditional financial institutions. But you know what is said about the devil and free meals? Again, in many parts of the world, such loan sharks (that's what they still are, only adorned in fancy suits and posh offices to appear respectable) go the extra lengths of sending life-threatening messages to individuals. The worst part is that they go on to access the phone books of debtors and send out messages to their contacts calling them all sorts of unprintable names and advising individuals not to have anything to do with them. This is a huge price to pay for debt, which has left many depressed and suicidal, leading to broken marriages and split families.

Reputation is too high a price to pay for debt. Once fractured, it takes the grace of God to put those pieces together again especially when the betrayal of trust is of a financial nature. I once read that God uses debts and pledges as metaphors for sin. In particular, He uses the metaphor of the cloak as a pledge as an explicit disobedience to His commands. His desire for you is that you don't compromise your dignity.

10. Financial Ruin

"Suddenly, your debtors will take action.
They will turn on you and take all you have,
while you stand trembling and helpless"
- Habakkuk 2:7, NIV

Financial ruin is always the pot of gold found not at the end but in the middle of the whirlwind, not the rainbow of debt. It is a monster that, when it roars, every part of you feels the tremor. One of my earliest childhood memories of witnessing financial ruin was that of a next-door neighbor whom we all grew to admire. He had choice vehicles, chauffeurs, and a home that distinctively stood out in the 80's in the neighborhood I grew up in.

I remember one morning waking up to hysterical shouts of nieghbours. We peered through our apartment windows to see strange men, accompanied by policemen. I saw the anguish on the faces of the family as their vehicles and other valuables were seized. Though naïve, it left a rotten feeling in the pit of my stomach. But at that age, I had limited knowledge that debt was responsible for the real-life soap opera we had just witnessed.

I also remember getting ready to have my second child, and like my first child, the plan was to have him in the USA. At that point, I was yet to inform Oduola of the drama that was to come. My prayer was to wake up one morning and find my bed all laid out by someone else for me to sleep in. I had depleted all our financial reserves and was literally living by the day, looking to God and her benevolence. I was ruined with no one to turn to but God and her. I still had a baby on the way who did not request his birth and who had to be taken care of.

Now, Oduola, my spouse, is a hard worker. Those who know her would testify without boundaries to this. She could work until the very last day if it were possible, but every man is expected not to be an infidel which is an inability to not provide. When I would be forced to open up about my financial ruin, we would elect to have the baby in a government medical facility, a far cry from her first pregnancy experience (absolutely nothing wrong with anyone using the same, just that where I am from, it's usually not a very pleasant experience). It would be a very uncomfortable birth process that would present more health challenges as a result of the fact that my finances were in tatters. After the birth of our son, it was a huge challenge and even more painful when you consider that this was months in the making and my baby wasn't delivered in a basket by a stork. A major risk of debt is that it will rip your finances to pieces, and the result is one that is a lot easier to read on the pages of this book than to live it.

11. Web of Broken Friendships/Ruined Relationships

*"An offended friend is harder to win back
than a fortified city. Arguments separate friends
like a gate locked with bars"*
- Proverbs 18:19, NIV

In the book "Shut Up and Listen" by Tillman Feritta, the owner of the NBA team, The Houston rockets, he describes the risk of having broken friendships and the wisdom he applied. "I know what exactly this feels like. When I was starting out, I tried to get my hands on money in every possible way I could—credit cards, you name it. (One thing I didn't do was reach out to friends for loans. If you want to lose a friend, just ask for a loan. Nothing destroys a friendship faster"

What you must recognize is that the greatest blessings you will come to enjoy under the heavens will come through men, and what debt systematically does is make a huge wreck of these conduit pipes of relationships. So that when your blessings or answered prayers seek expression, there are no men willing to transmit them to your earth realm due to the fact that debt has created very awful Grand Canyon rifts along the pathway between you and others.

They will likely recognize that it is much safer not to

associate with you for their well-being. They would keep a distance from anything that points to a potential association with a debtor who is not credible in words or actions. I have been clearly forsaken; I had friends who just dropped out of the radar completely. After all no one wanted to be associated with a debtor or someone with a credibility issue (thank you to those friends who never gave up, God bless them all). They did not want to be stained by virtue of association. When next you think of debt, you must remember the timeless adage, "Before borrowing from a friend, decide which you need the most."

Debt is a guaranteed relationship killer. Money hurts the union so badly that many never get to speak again to each other. In my opinion, this is one of the biggest risks to be considered. Debt is a garment, an appearance that can attract or repel fortune.

12. Health

"A Cheerful heart is good medicine,
but a broken spirit saps a person's strength."
- Proverbs 17:22, NIV

The biggest damage debt did to my health was having an impaired immune system. In other words, I was immunocompromised; the stress levels ensured I had a reduced capacity or ability to fight infections or any other diseases. It was open season for all bodily diseases for me. Due to the humongous stress, food lost its taste. I would go through the entire day on an empty tank before being forcefully prompted by my wife to eat. I literally looked pale from the multiple bashings I received from creditors, left, right, front, back, and centre, like an NFL footballer.

Every time I received some sort of demand, I felt like a professional boxer in a bout with my hands tied behind me. I had to receive all the blows without the ability to reply to any of the punches. It was debt that made me handicapped by tying both my hands behind my back, giving me an unfair advantage. I was sick to my soul, and it seemed like every phone call guaranteed endless headaches, and loose bowels. The headaches would sometimes lead to migraines. There was hardly anything that did seem to go right. I would remember getting a chicken pox infection at almost 40 and think to myself, oh no, this cannot be happening. It seemed even the slightest cold infection had me on a hospital bed. My spirit was broken, and a broken spirit dries up the bones.

If you want to know the greatest risk you run when you accept debt, it must be this: health. I have heard tales of people fighting ridiculous blood pressures, and it's all so surreal. Also, the damage to my mental health was also there. It took a great amount of wisdom to protect myself because you run the risk of being a real casualty and the earth continues to spin while you are long gone. The unbreakable bond or inseparable collaboration between debt and mental depression is not something to be handled with kid gloves. Once your mind is defeated, you have not only lost the battle to debt; you have lost the battle for life altogether. So, you want to pick up debt? Ask yourself if it is worth the price of your health.

13. Hurt to Family/Marriage

"One day the widow of a member of the
group of prophets came to Elisha and cried out,
"My husband who served you is dead, and you know how
he feared the Lord. But now a creditor has come
threatening to take my two sons as slaves."
- 2 Kings 4:1, NIV

Scripture speaks of the widow who came to Elisha in a desperate, last-minute attempt to attract succor. From the story, one thing is evident: despite his stated prophetic office, he died a debtor (showing again how debt ignores even your call, position, and anointing). And the sons of the widow may have spent their lives well trying to pay off a debt they possibly knew nothing of. Herein lies one of the drawbacks of this menace: it is unforgiving, even to unborn and future generations.

Hurt to my family is one of the biggest prices I would pay on the altar of debt. Oh, my family paid a number of prices. I robbed them of so much, and it was painful to watch. They were underserving participants in a complicated web of my errors. They were exposed to shame and ridicule. My wife must have taken the most of this, and for a long time, it took a toll on our communication and affected our marriage greatly.

I remember days when sex was not even on the cards to be considered. The mental space that should churn out sensual thoughts for my beloved wife was simply being choked by the cares of this world brought on by debt. It was tantamount to infidelity; though I was not cheating with another woman, I was cheating with the consequences of debt. I was so sucked into the drama; it affected everything, and I mean everything. I thought of scenarios: what if I was to die? I wasn't even thinking of legacy; what pain would my kids grow up in knowing I had failed them in accumulating debt for them to pay. You can pay with your marriage and family once debt becomes a factor in your affairs.

14. Expect the Drama

"The wicked snatch a widow's child from her breast,
taking the baby as security for a loan."
- Job 24:9, NIV

The unknown dropped calls at the weirdest hours, and the threat messages towards me and my family continued in bitter and quick succession. You must get ready to be responsible for everything that goes wrong in the lives of your creditors. Their problems become amplified due to your indebtedness. The truth is that humans need an outlet for issues and are quick to connect the dots when there are individuals tied to the misfortune they face.

Every single thing that went wrong in the life of a creditor was my fault. Now I take responsibility, knowing there is a far-reaching ripple effect when debt matters arise. It was really draining emotionally to know everything was my fault, whether it was correct or not. Drama usually followed closely when this occurred. I once had a creditor sit at my front gate, insisting he wouldn't leave until he got paid. It took God's special grace to persuade him to leave. The choice of going into debt plays a short-term game at the expense of the massive winnings of the long game.

EIGHT DAYS TO REMEMBER

A WEEK OF RECKONING

In the last chapter I spoke about the risks of debt, and tried to highlight the various risks you run when you get in bed with debt. There were many incidents in the course of my journey out of debt. One particular event stands out for me, and I felt I should give it a whole chapter for more clarity, emphasis and impact.

My goal is to further drum down the ear drums, how playing with debt is akin to playing with fire. You could get burnt slightly or badly, either way, you feel the intense pain. When I had to face the browbeat of debt and understand how it intimidates and frightens into powerless submission, induces fear, reduces the spirit to a state where it is broken, and all courage lost, I knew I was dealing with a special class and kind of monster.

By now, I want to run with the assumption that you agree that there are real consequences to having any form of relationship with debt, and if you are still sitting on the fence, understand that I had a taste of this bread of doom, and it troubled me for a long period of time. It has taken the divine grace of God for me to understand the reason for the scars, and this has helped me through the phase of healing and recovery. Enjoy my tale.

I had just retired to bed after dinner and had my wife later join me. If my memory serves me correctly, we probably even might have gone through a steamy conjugal session; everything preceding what I am about to narrate became a blur. Now, I have a team of amazing professionals who help in the running of my home/office so as to make things more convenient for my wife and me. It wasn't Sunday, my driver, or chauffeur who appeared at the front door of my modest home to pick up my son to school. The nanny was probably half asleep and, almost in a robotic manner, opened the door, I am sure, without bothering to first look into the door's peephole to see who it was.

Permit me to quickly take you back a few weeks to this incident for perspective on God's loving role in my affairs: So, my young son, Chris Jr., woke up quite roughly and proceeded to my bedroom to inform me of a nightmare. His customary action is to enter my room, switch on the lights, and shake me without a care or concern in the world. I remember sitting in bed as he recounted his dream. "I dreamt that some men came into the house, they said they were policemen and took you away. I could see the tears building up in his sleepy eyes, wiping them away. I assured him while stealing a glance at my now fully awake wife, "Don't worry, daddy will be fine, and if ever he gets taken away, be sure that daddy will always come back home to you." I was unsure how much assurance my few words gave the young lad, but I felt a strong drowning feeling in the pit of my stomach—something sinister was coming.

Back to the initial story...

On that fateful Tuesday morning, there was no sign of the early morning dew announced by the chirping birds, indicating the passing away of the dark night, would birth anything different. The same clockwork scene that had happened every day occurred, only this time with a curious twist. The stark difference this time was that it wasn't Sunday at the door knocking. If only the nanny had made use of the front door peephole, she would have seen the armed policemen and officers of a crime commission, and would have probably given me some advance warning (I played the scenario so many times).

The ease of entry into my home meant they effortlessly marched the nanny, who would have been scared out of her wits, up my stairs to my bedroom door. Now, living in a home with mostly females and two young sons whose voices couldn't rise above a few decibels, one could only imagine the unfamiliar fear on the face of my wife and myself when we heard a loud baritone voice ordering us to open the door. Requesting who they were, they introduced themselves as law enforcement, with an instruction to invite me to their commission.

I requested time to dress up while giving instructions to my wife, who was at this time already up to speed with every creditor and all my financial dealings. I also told her to contact my lawyer and close family members. I gave her a tensed kiss on the forehead, unsure of where this grid-like road would lead. Being a lawyer, I understood quite clearly how the lines between a civil matter (such as a transaction gone wrong) could be interpreted as a criminal matter by law enforcement whose driving desire is the petition before them and, in most cases, not the truth and sincerity of parties involved.

I followed the armed guards and officers into a waiting bus tailed by a black tinted Range Rover that must have played a role in identifying my home. I gave no further notice to it, said my daily prayers internally, and resigned to the promises of God in Isaiah 43. My phones were taken off me, and there I began a journey to the unknown, like Odysseus of legend upon Poseidon's sea.

The white Toyota Hiace bus snaked around the busy Lagos metropolis for some time. No words were exchanged at this time. The uniformed men decided to intensify the suspense by temporarily embracing the code of silence akin to Omertà. I did my best to steady my head, but my mind wandered rambunctiously through a thousand scenarios or more.

I prayed for peace and calmness internally and heaven dispatched an answer in record time. So, I finally decided to break the silence by picking up a conversation with all the individuals in the vehicle who expressed surprise at my relative calmness. I responded that the only crime was a business transaction gone wrong and a firm commitment to repay, so therein was the confidence.

We arrived at the Lagos office of the officials. I was instructed to remain in the vehicle. After a wait of about fifteen minutes, in a lightning change of countenance, I was informed that I was to be taken from Lagos to Ibadan, a city in another state, some 118 km by road. I insisted on making a call to my family to inform them, a request that was granted, and the utter shock expressed by all I informed was evident. It was a well-orchestrated operation, and clearly there was a puppet master pulling the strings behind the stage curtains.

We sojourned on the notorious Lagos/Ibadan expressway. Where the officials decided they were hungry, they stopped by a roadside bukka (a local Nigerian street restaurant). I declined the offer of what must have been a stomach-filling meal for them. Choosing to tangibly gauge the situation before any comfort, the reality would hit when I would request to make use of the toilet and realized my freedom had been taken away when an official held guard outside while I answered nature's call.

The "interrogation" in the vehicle continued as the journey resumed. I noticed there was a strategy to extract information, which I played along with. I was in debt and still couldn't fathom how I had metamorphosed into a criminal in the eyes of the person on the receiving end of my indebtedness.

On arrival at the final destination a few hours later, I stepped out of the bus into the administrative office of the commission, where glances amongst their colleagues revealed their glee at another fish in their net. From then on, the interrogations intensified, my lawyer would soon arrive, and I was treated to a barrage of questions on the facts of the petition. By which time I had been given the opportunity to read, and seeing a description of me in those pages of black and white is something I will never forget.

I would be grilled for over 5 hours and made to write countless statements of my side of the story. I must admit that, beyond the language used by the other party, I pretty much owned up to my debt and explained steps I had taken to liquidate it. After questioning being a lawyer, I was aware that the next issue on the table would be bail. I requested those conditions and wasn't surprised at the unrealistic demands to be met. I relaxed my spirit to prepare for whatever was to come. Afterwards, there was a quick walk to the detention centre, and I shared some last few words with my lawyer, this happened in seconds. The iron doors were opened, and I walked into a different world. I was now classified as a "suspect" in all my dealings during my stay.

I was made to initially stay at the reception of the detention centre due to the kindness of the officer on duty and based on the mood of the officers on duty. The next eight days would see me sleep on a flat-out, bed bug-infested mattress in the same single set of clothes I was picked up in. The discomfort was nothing compared to the mental agony of what my wife, kids, and family were going through.

I regretted not picking a book or anything that could keep me company and would serve as a tranquilizer for my mental space. There were whirlwinds of conflicting thoughts in my head. My soul trembled vigorously, like a high-tension cable beaten by a strong wind. I would find a mangled copy of the Bible, with several of its pages torn out by past suspects. I would presume many held on to those pages for sanity and comfort during their individual travails involving many interrogation sessions or visits to court. What remained of the Bible had incoherent scribbles of the desperation and heartfelt cries of those who had previously held on to it. I tried my best to catch up with my word study and covered considerable ground. It is interesting how much you get done when you have nothing else to do.

Another impression was how suspects had to remove any form of string or rope from their clothing. With our clothes loosely fitting, we all appeared like American rappers would in a typical music video. Every single piece of jewelry was taken from us. Prior to this experience, I could count the number of times my wedding band ever came off my finger. I was forced to take the customary mug shot for what would be a possible conviction. With fingerprints and biometrics taken, it was evident that, with my kind of debt, I was guilty before even proven innocent.

I took the picture smiling and remembered several stories I had read of those in similar circumstances whose stories became blog headlines, viral social media conversations, and the whole nine yards. The irony of it all was that the gentleman taking the picture would comment on my calm demeanor, and I knew it could only have been divinely sponsored.

Though I was gasping for breath like a man fully sunken in mud, the Holy Spirit was always present during every step of this ordeal. He fortified me from within, bestowing upon me a voice and a serenity I never imagined I could possess. He would go on to rid my heart of any bitterness, pain, and anger. Indeed, it is noteworthy how light you feel when you allow Him to lift off your shoulders, burdens that are seemingly impossible to bear. They would place me in a cramped cell with tiny rooftop windows. That was the only indication of what time of day or what season it was. Often, when suspects stepped out, the most important piece of information you could return with was what time of the day it was.

The average cell was housing at various times between 15 to 23 inmates. All were held from the smallest to the biggest infractions. Filled with bed bug-infested mattresses, sleeping on the bare floor was not any better. The bathroom and toilets were a story on their own, as expected. The mood in the cells was often very positive. I eventually realized God was placing me here for something, and I had to be sensitive to arrest the moment. I would experience my first prison evangelism, and the highlight was leading a young man to Christ. His early morning prayers, though very silent and hardly audible, would touch me. Upon further conversations, we would realize the mistakes that we all made that made us inmates in the first place. I assured him of hope and did my best to lift the spirits of others by offering pro-bono legal services. It echoed the importance of being led by the Spirit to avoid finding yourself in a financial mess.

Visiting times were also a major feature, and while I received none from my family, who, just like the early church, were making supplications, it was heartbreaking to see the wives, and children of suspects, filled with tears and hopelessness. The uncertainty of what was to come was etched across their faces and was a pointer to the disastrous effects of our decisions on not just us but our loved ones especially. I would watch parents cry and bemoan their lot in the grand scheme of life while giving their family members small amounts of money to purchase what they could. While at the same time giving feedback from lawyers and well wishes.

I spent a total of eight days in what is known among inmates as the hole hotel. For those eight days, mealtimes were torture. With my very sensitive and potentially loose bowels, I couldn't run the risk of having an upset stomach or picking up any infection. I was forced to begin a compulsory water fast, giving up my meal allocation to others who were more than glad to feast on any bonus serving. Since what was served most times hardly did any justice to the hunger pangs,.

Expectedly, my health took a downturn, especially since I was roommates with rodents, insects, bugs, and millions, if not zillions, of other micro-organisms not visible to human eyes. I coughed for many days and was taken to the sick bay for checks. The antibiotics did not do much, and it was a real risk to anyone's health to be in such an environment for such a prolonged period of time.

The only source of entertainment for the young adults were television screens positioned outside the bars of the cell. That would have had suspects argue back on what to watch between saucy music videos that got them so excited, old Asian Kung Fu movies, and sports. The writings and graffiti on the walls of the cells provided a generous peek into the thinking of those who had previously occupied them. From motivational quotes to political statements, to coarse vulgarity to religious philosophies, it had it all. For what it's worth, there is nothing poetic or glorious about being confined behind the cold steel bars of prison.

When the episode was over, I was asked to have a reconciliation meeting with my creditor. I understood better that, after 8 days, I needed to share the tales of my experience. Though it seemed I had lost 8 days of my life, in retrospect, I realized I had gained a lifetime of experience for my own personal evolution, growth, and development as a person to correct my ways and, more importantly, to share with others the potential risks they will suffer when they become friends with debt.

It could lead to more ruin than you can fathom, and even though I was able to get through it and a number of debtors have a fairy tale ending to their debt journey, it is a harsh fact that debt has cost many the most important thing they have, their lives. A price definitely not worth paying.

Eight days seemed like eight months. The racy mental and psychological plunge I took into the deepest recesses of my being was something that shaped me for life. In those eight days, I had moments of clarity and truth: All that had happened was my fault, and only I could work towards making things right. Reminiscing on what I just went through, one of the best feelings I had leaving that place, stepping out through the doors as I went past the armed personnel who had kept guard over the past week, was the fact that I left with no anger or bitterness towards anyone. I would rather build a steely resolve to arise on my two feet and face the monster of debt head-on. No more mess; I vowed under God!

CHAPTER 5

25 STRATEGIC ACTIONS TO TAKE WHEN IN DEBT

*"When you are married
to your mistakes, you will continue
to deliver regrets."*

Paul Enenche
Nigerian Pastor, Author, and Musician

Debt is like a faulty computer algorithm that needs to be rewritten from scratch, and this important action will take a lot of commitment, or more importantly, discipline, to execute. Like a mentor, Jim Rohn would say, "It's either the pain of discipline or the pain of regret."

If you have gotten this far in this book, it's clear evidence that you are seeking a way out of the debt quagmire that you or circumstances have created. You should understand that there is no magic lamp you can rub to summon a mystical genie, nor is there a secret cave where you can mine free gold and instantly eliminate debt. Rather, it would take strategic actions for you to escape. It's akin to a gazelle evading a hunter's grasp or a bird dodging a net.

If you are reading this and you know you are skating on thin ice, which without a moment's notice may all cave in, it is time to stop and embrace some wisdom. Recognize there is hope for redemption and a fresh start if you are ready to put in the necessary work.

Debt is like a huge pile of ice, which will surely melt away in the face of the scorching heat of financial responsibility. It may take time to pay it all off, depending on the degree of debt owed, but the beauty is who you become in the process of redemption. I tell you, going through redemption from debt is priceless. So put yourself together, lay all ego aside, make a commitment to see this through, and start the process TODAY!

Like Proverbs 6:4 (Msg) advocates,

> *"Friend don't waste a minute,*
> *get yourself out of that mess."*

Take the following steps highlighted in this book, and you will need a telescope to view the debt from yesterday. These steps are enumerated as follows:

1. Accept your Mistakes, Believe Strongly that Debt Can and Will End, and Put in the Work

> *"Faith is the confidence that what*
> *we hope for will actually happen; it gives us*
> *assurance about things we cannot see."*
> *- Hebrews 11:1, NIV*

The very first step I took was to sincerely accept my mistakes and own them (this book is another testimony to that). This singular action became the turning point in my bitter debt odyssey. This action ensures debt loses its stranglehold and death grip on you. Honestly, when I was in debt, I could not see any light at the end of the tunnel, no matter what was being told me. I was blinded to any possibility of freedom.

The first step in your liberation walk must arise from a place of faith, a deep-rooted belief that you can and will be debt-free. The absence of this almost makes it impossible to begin this journey. Now I admit that most times back then, even faith did not make any sense and left me so uncomfortable. But I had to learn to trust in Him, who is all-wise yet invisible. I liken faith in your journey to freedom from debt to the ignition in a motor vehicle. Now it does not matter if it's a Ferrari or a pay loader; the truth is that without turning the key or pushing the ignition, that engine will remain static despite the horsepower it possesses. Action is thus the much-needed spark plug to initiate your exodus from the dark shores of debt land.

Once you are not just content to conjure up the thought of freedom but also ready to act on it, there immediately appears on the horizon a realm for your being financially buoyant, free from lenders, taking care of others, and being a blessing to your generation and the world at large. You will realize all the belief systems that guarantee your freedom will suddenly come alive to ensure things graduate from a mental state to a physical reality. It is for this reason that our belief systems are so powerful and can determine the outcome of our lives. After all, as a man thinks, he is (Proverbs 23:7)!

To become debt-free, your positive debt-free belief system must align with the steps you would take to grant you your desire. So, it starts with a belief. My question is, do you want to be free from debt? Remember, this is not an excuse for laziness; beliefs are powerful, and do you want to know what is even more powerful? Actions taken to activate these beliefs?

2. Re-dedication to Your Core Positive Principles and Values

Another firm decision that you should take is something I have gleaned from the bestselling book, "H3 Leadership" by Brad Lomenick, the lead visionary and President of Catalyst, one of America's largest movements of next generation leaders.

What happens when you compromise on your principles and values, just like I did? Apart from apologizing and making amends, remember that it is never too late to recommit to your principles. Trust may be compromised and relationships damaged, but that doesn't mean that your convictions are irrelevant. Remember, even big ships with big failures can return from the abyss.

You must make a decision to rise like a phoenix and rededicate the remainder of your life not to repeat the same mistakes, to discard faulty principles and values, and to pick up those that align with who you are meant to be and start living according to their dictates. The principles and values are as unique as your fingerprint, so make a conscious effort to rediscover and go on to recreate the best version of yourself.

3. Let the Sunlight Come into Your Life

"Imole de o, okunkun parada."
(When light comes, darkness disappears)
- Dunsin Oyekan
Nigerian Gospel Singer and Songwriter

Whenever I remember the thick darkness, the threat letters, emails, calls from creditors, law enforcement agents, and lawyers, and how I would go out of my way to hide the demands from those closest to me, I remember the series of books, which I call my journals of debt. In retrospect, I laughed, but in those moments, it was not funny at all. My life felt as though heavy black curtains were always covering me, preventing me from seeing the light.

I failed to understand and appreciate the power of light, literally. The biggest lie debt will tell you is for you to keep everything a secret and tell no one. This may seem to buy some temporary relief, but it is never sustainable, only empowering your ego while you plunge deeper into the murky shaft of mess.

I came across a remarkable book by Matt Keller, titled "God of the Underdogs," which contains a phrase that has the power to shatter the long-standing barriers I had allowed to conceal my debt, thereby enabling it to flourish and control me. He said, "Whatever stays in the dark grows in its power over you, but whatever is brought into the light lessens its power over you."

At that point, I realized it was time to let the sun's rays in. I would go on to gradually share my challenges and problems with those closest to me, and rather than the expected rebuke, shame, and embarrassment, I received understanding, love, support, and prayers. This was a major freedom—one I had never experienced since the journey began.

The minute the light came in, the darkness of debt gradually lost its power and unshackled me from the fear that had been my prison guard/warden for years. Though I had tasted what it meant to be in physical confinement, I realized I was the victim of a bigger and more vicious prison—the one I built with my own hands, which was reinforced by my keeping it a secret!

If you find yourself in debt, this should be the very first step to take on the staircase of redemption, and it will split open the curtains over your finances and let the sunlight come in. This goes along with the clarity, fresh air, and health benefits you need to be set free.

So, today, let the sunlight come in!

4. Take It One Day At A Time

"Therefore, do not worry about tomorrow,
for tomorrow will worry about itself. Each day
has enough trouble of its own."
– Matthew 6:34, NIV

This was very tough to execute but definitely worth it, and as I personally have discovered, very achievable. There is always going to be a strong temptation to try and overthink your days. I remember how many times I would be lying awake in bed while the rest of the world slept. I would be listening to the eerie rhythms from the bowels of midnight. Sometimes, mosquitoes would conduct grating operas in my ears. I would stare at the ceilings, wondering what new drama the day would present, what new insults I was to receive, and what new threats would confront my freedom. It was a free-for-all mental royal rumble (reminiscent of the wrestling bouts of the 1980s and '90s World Wrestling Federation). It took a determined and prayerful effort for me to adopt a radical stance. I initially felt guilty that, by relaxing, I was being too insensitive to the demands of creditors who were inconvenienced. But I soon discovered that was just another lie I was living. I needed to be alive and well to offset my debts!

You are not to worry too much about tomorrow, which happens to be a small footnote in the annals of time that you clearly have no control over or assurance that you will even see. The harsh truth is that tomorrow always takes care of itself, whatever it brings. Know this and know the truth so that you can rest!

You must endeavour to take it exactly the way God intended, which is one day at a time, and nothing more or less. This is not to say you should not plan, or be responsive, but it's the consciousness of knowing the limits and drawing the lines that guarantees you are firmly balanced on the ground. Remember, you can only do what is permitted for you to do. You will suffer great physical, emotional, and mental wrecks if you flout this principle. Therefore, take it one day at a time.

5. Put the Season to Great Use

*"So, David left Gath and escaped to
the cave of Adullam, soon his brothers and
all his other relatives joined him there. Then others
began coming– men who were in trouble or **in debt**
or who were just discontented until David
was the captain of about 400 men."*
- 1 Samuel 22:1-2, NLT emphasis added

Every time I reflect on the importance of down times, I just smile because I am blessed to have unlocked and understood their power firsthand. Those seasons are usually impregnated with possibilities for you to explore and, with the passage of time, for you to express. You won't be holding this book in your hands if I did not decide to put the season of my debt journey to good use. Once I discovered the lessons, I continued to learn as I went along. So, I made up my mind to transform this all into a very effective lesson for anyone who is battling the monster of debt. I made it a matter of duty to capture my thoughts, experiences, and lessons in writing to ensure no one who comes into contact with me or this material would have to lose to the debt monster again.

During this season, which is likened to hiding in the cave of Adullam, there is often a state of paralysis of sorts. One is stripped, wholly, to their barest minimum. Many times, I was unsure of what to do. And when I knew it, just like David did, I realized it was usually the perfect season for training and a potential reset.

It is a golden opportunity to build capacity and rejig the foundations to guarantee capacity for higher heights. I particularly love the fact that the men referenced in the Scripture above were just as I was—in deep debt! So, it's nothing new. The men needed an escape channel from their overwhelming impossibilities. A place where they could make sense of their circumstances and engage the possibilities overhead. A place where they would not bemoan their faith or struggle with the stinging impression of others who had labelled them with uncharitable tags.

During this season, they went far away from the crowds and strategically positioned themselves under David's mentorship and leadership. Their season of debt was put to not just good use but great use, and they would emerge from the rubble of their ordeal as "David's Mighty Men of Valour." The same discontented debtors were the warriors who fought to establish and stabilize the country of Israel, and from all biblical historical accounts, it was not bad for a band of misfits who once writhed in the fetters of debt.

6. Mind Renewal

*We use our powerful God-given tools to smash
down barriers erected against the truth of God,
fitting every loose thought, emotion, and impulse
into the structure of life shaped by Christ.*
- 2 Corinthians 10:5, Msg

Like I have previously established, debt is a mindset. So, since it's a paradigm—a sustained way of thinking you have reinforced with your actions over a period of time—you can also make a conscious decision to have a total renewal in the way you think and reason. A creditor once gave me a powerful, unsolicited piece of advice: "That the same amount of energy it takes to get into debt is proportional to the same energy it would take to get productive and stay debt-free."

Many see no other doorway to go through than the door with the bold sign, DEBT, crested on it. Everything else seems to appear like a brick wall. Don't be too harsh on yourself if you have found yourself in this state. I once thought in this unproductive way and can guarantee you that there are countless other opportunities available to you. But first, there must be a renewal of your mind and how you analyze situations and act on the result of such analysis.

The scripture above remains a potent indicator of how to

achieve powerful results. Many of us have what I would describe as loose thoughts, emotions, and impulses that serve obediently only the purposes of debt and nothing more in terms of profitable productivity. In my personal journey, I discovered that it was when I mirrored the life and character of Christ, his mindset and orientation towards life, and specifically when it came to debt and money, that my actions equally corresponded. Then my life began to change to reflect the renewed mindset I was cultivating.

Debt, like a dark cloud, began to clear away. When in debt, you must always encourage yourself; discouragement is destructive. Always remember that your life is a byproduct of the way you think. Think past debt and decide today to start thinking about and living with financial freedom.

7. Financial Knowledge Overhaul

"I will instruct you,
and teach you in the way you should go;
I will counsel you and watch over you."
- Psalm 32:8, NIV

I lacked sufficient financial knowledge to handle my business and personal financial matters. My inability to acknowledge this insufficiency and seek help guaranteed financial mishaps and inevitable debt. Today, there is ample financial information and tools at your disposal to help you gain financial knowledge. The bulk of which is available at the click of a button.

There are individuals who are proven veterans, many of whom have overcome debt themselves and give financial tips to guarantee their freedom. One of my personal favorites must be Dave Ramsey, who is an American radio personality and personal finance personality with a mission to help individuals sail their financial ships through his Ramsey Show, books, and other tools. Two of his hugely popular tools are the Seven Baby Steps and the Snow Ball Debt Repayment.

You can intentionally seek out individuals who appeal to you and will guide you during this much-needed overhaul. Financial literacy is a must and a necessity you cannot jettison. Not only will the literacy help you identify steps to becoming debt-free, it will more importantly keep you free, as you will get to understand that many individuals in a lifetime face several cycles of debt.

8. Identify and Note Down All Debts and Creditors

Imagine an individual who is unable to swim and drowns. He or she would require calmness not to go under the waves by conserving sufficient energy and being frugal with their use of oxygen.

That's exactly what I want you to do: stay calm. Get a journal if you don't have one, and start what I would call an honest appraisal of your present financial position. It can be very revealing and challenging, but also hugely therapeutic. Despite the huge size of the debt on your shoulders, you will realize that the figure can still be captured in a single line on a sheet of paper. Whatever can be written down can be conquered.

You should start by listing all the debts that you owe, from the smallest to the largest. Add the names and contacts of the creditors. With this exercise, you are able to know how deep the pit really is, erasing any assumptions or guesses. Remember that you can easily break a single broom stick on its own, but you will find it nearly impossible to break an entire broom bunch.

The next exercise, though extremely tough but absolutely necessary, is to start the uncomfortable process of reaching out to those creditors you have on your list (at least those that will grant you an audience). Express your challenges in keeping with agreed-upon terms with extreme humility laced with sincerity. Affirm your intention to be honourable to pay back your debt, every single dime owed, and also communicate after extensive planning when this would be. Since they won't want to be in the dark about your plans.

You must understand that when in debt, honest communication is the golden key. No creditor likes a debtor, and even worse, one that doesn't communicate, no matter how awful things are. Going through this step may give you some reprieve in the hands of a few individuals or companies. Thus, we are buying you the much-needed time to think objectively and pragmatically about the strategic steps you must take to win back your freedom from debt. Remember that as long as you owe, you are a prisoner. Also remember this golden rule at this stage: don't make commitments to creditors you know you cannot fulfil, no matter how tempting they may appear. Whatever peace you may extract is always short-lived, and not keeping your word would further damage any credibility you have left. It will further complicate things along the way to your liberty.

9. Stop Borrowing

"The Lord your God will bless you as He has promised.
You will lend money to many nations, but you will never
need to borrow; you will rule over many nations,
but they will not rule over you."
- Deuteronomy 15:6, NIV

When in debt, you must do all it humanly takes to get out of it, and one of the most strategic moves is for you to STOP BORROWING. When you are in a big hole, the first way out is to stop anything that even remotely sounds or looks like digging.

The writer, Molly Ivins, rightfully captures it this way:

> *"The first rule of holes; when*
> *you are in one, stop digging."*

With every hole you dig, what is needed is more sand to cover it up, and that, my friend, is the simple definition of insanity, aka madness.

But you are not alone, and you don't need to beat yourself too hard on this. I personally know the relief of being able to shut my eyes for a day after buying that extra time. But it is usually short-lived and leads to more drama further down the road. You must fight and overcome the seductive temptation of robbing Peter to pay Paul. I encountered this challenge on multiple occasions. I took from one person to pay another until I was caught up in a giant maze of financial conundrums. It is an ineffective and impossible way to discharge debt and leaves you in the cold, tentacular grip of the debt octopus. Debt is and will always be a poor choice. Quick to borrow and slow to pay are usually the results. Do not rob Peter to pay Paul. Again, by all means, STOP BORROWING!

10. Tackle the Interest Monster with the Biggest Chains

*"Usury once in control
will wreck the nation."*
- William Lyon Mackenzie King

Have you ever seen a river or sea with extreme currents? It is always a scary proposition if you are forced to swim from one side to the other, even if the possibility of freedom exists on the other side.

Interest is like swimming against the tide, running uphill on a rocky mountain, or trying to hit the bull's-eye target that is always in motion. Interest almost always guarantees your inability to have a clear, concise picture of what you are aiming to conquer. I remember several times that I missed payment deadlines and had to bear the undiscounted indignation of creditors. Interest penalties would guarantee my being violently evacuated from a deeper hole and into a whirlpool. I felt like I was in a maze of quick-rotating masses of water, and the rising currents worsened my ability to make sense of my situation.

If you seek to get out of your own peculiar financial whirlpool, you must first identify the debts that have the most crushing interests. This is a necessity that must occur because it will guarantee you the clarity and peace that are needed to tackle the remainder of your debt portfolio. Tackling this interest monster will help you lock in your debt target before giving you the clarity to deploy your repayment missile for maximum impact. If you ever played with a balloon, you would realize that the more air it holds, the higher it can fly. It is similar to interest, which acts as air to your debt balloon, which, if not quickly pricked, could see things get out of your reach and out of control.

11. Pay Those with 'Amazing' Temperaments

*"A prudent person foresees danger
and takes precautions. The simpleton goes blindly
on and suffers the consequences."*
- Proverbs 27:12, NIV

Prudent: wise or judicious in practical affairs; discreet or circumspect; sagacious

One of my favourite books, which I read while growing up in school, was the popular 1945 satirical allegorical novella by George Orwell entitled "Animal Farm." It tells the creative story of a group of mischievous farm animals who rebel against their human owner, hoping to create a utopian society where all the animals can be equal, free, and happy. Ultimately, the rebellion is betrayed by a number of elements, and the farm ends up in a state that is worse than it was before under a pig named Napoleon. One of the famous farm commandments that is forever enshrined in my mind is the golden rule: "All animals are equal, but some are more equal than others."

One personal rule I have always stood by is that no creditor is wrong; after all, I approached them without any coercion, hat in hand, agreeing to their terms. My personal experience, on the other hand, of dealing with debt also showed me that, just like in the story of Animal Farm, in the real world, not all creditors are equal. You would find that creditors possess a wide array of temperaments that would be unabashedly displayed when pushed to the wall by your indebtedness. From those who will show so much positive consideration for your present position to others for whom it is just business and nothing else and will be willing to tear down the world to get the clothes off your back and possibly give your family away in slavery like in ancient times to settle your debt with them.

While their recovery may seem justifiable to balance their books and suffer no loss, which is a fair argument, the tactics employed are sometimes the most draconian, to say the least. Some would show compassion and understanding; others won't, and you can't and shouldn't judge. My candid presentation is that life is just like the Animal Farm, where not all the animals are equal. Some will bring you down; others may give you time. Quite a number of creditors will approach law enforcement, the courts, or other judicial means to settle their score with you. This is, more often than not, a process you don't ever want to be entangled in. Little wonder the Scriptures advocate settling this amazing group.

Matthew 5:25-26 (NLT) says,

When you are on the way to court with
your adversary, settle your differences quickly.
Otherwise, your accuser may hand you over
to the judge, who will hand you over to an officer,
and you will be thrown into prison. And if
that happens, you surely won't be free again
until you have paid the last penny.

When there is silence from such creditors, don't take this as an opportunity to let down your guard. You must be on red alert at all times. With the wisdom that everything and anything may be sprung on you.

After a careful review of all your creditors, it is important that you weigh them all on a scale based on your past dealings with them and after you have approached them all with the best intentions vis-à-vis your financial state. The feedback will help you rip off the mask on your creditors and point you in the direction of the exact steps to take, and this can be achieved by being prudent in your observation of their personalities.

12. Decisions

*"Whoever disregards discipline comes
to poverty and shame, but whoever heeds
correction is honored."*
- Proverbs 13:18, NIV

When it comes to debt, escaping from it is the only wise and firm decision you must make. Not a thought but a firm decision, which I liken to a nexus or union of thoughts and actions.

Proverbs 6:5 (NLT) gives the action we can adopt for anyone who finds themselves in debt.

*"Save yourself like a gazelle escaping
from a hunter, like a bird fleeing from a net."*

You probably watched one of those exciting National Geographic programmes on the Animal Kingdom and have seen those gazelles doing their best to escape from a predator that is positioned to strike and kill. Or maybe it's a bird that mistakenly gets caught in a hunter's net. There is a common trait they all possess that can guarantee their survival, and that is their desperation to be free.

To be debt-free, you must make a desperate decision to be free from both the hunter and the net. I remember making this decision to be free, and it was the best I ever made on my debt journey. I realized I couldn't afford to be relaxed or comfortable with my pathetic state. I was in a quagmire, and I needed my entire being to be in synchrony with the decision to be desperate and to be free. A man who is drowning is so desperate for oxygen, and that's the situation you are in when in debt. You are drowning not in water but in a cesspool of financial mess, and you must breathe to survive. Therefore, your survival is based on a decision to be debt-free.

13. Get Timely Professional Assistance

"Plans go wrong for lack of advice;
many advisers bring success."
- Proverbs 15:22, NIV

I smiled when it got to this advice nugget part. I cast my mind back to how fortunate I was to adopt this and reach out for professional help, not the emotional "everything is going to be all right" type. But I came into contact with experienced individuals in their respective fields of endeavour who possessed what it took to get me out of debt. I had read an amazing book on debt written by a friend who was a financial advisor and debt expert with many years of experience finding her way through the harsh, unforgiving jungle of debt. That one divinely orchestrated phone call I put across to the author would resurrect a belief that I could also be free.

The first advice I got, amongst so many others, as time progressed, was the need to speak to a lawyer, which was to ward off, where possible and necessary, the tsunami demand of creditors. I would go on to engage a lawyer who I was led to in my spirit, and he would go on to be a shield that was much needed and will forever be appreciated. The transparency was a breath of fresh air, and having someone willing to go to battle for me was really invigorating and encouraging. He approached several creditors based on temperament, interests, etc. and made appeals for renegotiations of terms, requests for time, and other offers to protect me from damaging actions taken by creditors. I cannot overemphasize the need for professional help; though some may cost you money and convenience, it is an investment that would save you much more down the road.

Such individuals must be persons of repute who you know can rise to the occasion when the volcano erupts by putting in a good word for you (since most times, at this point, yours is no longer considered bankable). This will help to prevent certain decisions taken by creditors, which can be damaging and sometimes irreversible.

The scripture in Proverbs 15:1 (NLT) states:

"A gentle answer deflects anger,
but harsh words make tempers flare."

They usually should be wise individuals able to offer godly, wholesome, productive advice, especially individuals who have experienced or have navigated a financial crisis or debt at some point in their lives. Their words are a powerful tonic in this season to ensure you don't give up. You can also access resources such as books and videos by experienced professionals who can serve as captains to help you navigate through stormy seas. This is a life-challenging experience. In my case, some of these individuals were at my beck and call through books, messages, and online videos. They are still there waiting for you; their kind words, described aptly in Proverbs 16:24 (NLT), will be like 'honey—sweet to the soul and healthy for the body', just what the doctor recommends.

14. Accept that Nobody Owes You Anything

This is a very harsh truth. You must unquestionably accept this immovable fact: 'nobody owes you anything.'

Many fail to appreciate that ego is the greatest enemy of the human soul. There was always a tendency for me to expect so much assistance from other people, and when I did not receive what I sought, hubris or excessive pride would set in, and the disadvantage is that it served as dust in my eyes.

The arrogance of believing that I deserved the help or assistance I needed from others to save me from the mess I personally created was foolhardy. Looking retrospectively, it makes me feel naive and elicits a chuckle, thinking about the overconfidence displayed. You must purge yourself of any self-entitled expectation; any support you get to assist you, take it as a blessing. Not family, not friends—no one owes you anything to sort yourself out. With the tips in this book, you have all the keys to being debt-free, and if by happenstance assistance comes, be grateful and keep it moving.

Human beings are not what you think, as my mentor, Apostle Joshua Selman, would stress, "People really don't care that much about you; they are passionately obsessed with making meaning of their own lives."

Also remember, we live in a cold world; therefore, don't be deceived; not everyone wants to see you free. Many enjoy and delight in seeing others struggle; it gives them a high of some sort. I believe this is a worthy strategy because many labour longer to become debt-free due to the emotional hit they suffer from the lack of support or help when in debt.

15. Learn to Kick Shame to the Curb

*"Instead of your shame you will have
a double portion, and instead of humiliation
they will shout for joy over their portion."*
- Isaiah 61:7, NASB

Oh boy! The shame—the gruelling shame—that debt brought along with it. Shame, like most emotions, is perceived differently by humans, so the shame I experienced is most likely not going to be the same as yours. You are in debt, so it is time for serious readjustment because it is not going to be business as usual. I quite vividly remember many occasions when I would be making mental mathematical gymnastics due to the prices of items in a grocery store while walking across the aisle. I was very much aware of what I had in my bank account. There were times I would substitute items looking for a cheaper brand or, even more damaging to my health or that of a loved one, a cheaper drug due to my financial situation.

A few times, I would be at the till and be quite sure that I would be unable to afford all I had picked up in my trolley. Making notes of what was a necessity or a want, and having a cashier visibly irritated at my slow pace and holding up the queue. I got invited to several business breakfast meetings or lunch meet-ups, and before attending, I would ensure I was well fed from home to avoid the temptation of splurging and having to pay a much more painful price afterwards, long after the dessert had been long digested. The most painful experiences for me had to do with health care. Nothing is more punishing than having a loved one down with sickness and the inability to afford proper healthcare. Most of these experiences, as you would expect, would prop up shame without a doubt. But I had to overcome and kick shame to the curb because the impression of others over a situation that had overwhelmed me was not for me to lose sleep over. Especially since this wasn't my permanent station in life. One of the ways to overcome debt is to truly avoid shameful emotions, which could drown you, make you ineffective, and ensure you remain in debt.

16. Lifestyle Change

"A single rebuke does more
for a person of understanding than a hundred
lashes on the back of a fool."
- Proverbs 17:10, NIV

A famous adage goes like this: It's always a matter of time before 'a fool and his money are soon parted'. There is a vital need for prioritization in your lifestyle when grappling with debt, and there is no way you can truly be debt-free if you sustain the very lifestyle pattern that got you into debt in the first place. Man is a creature of habit; therefore, this may be one of the most difficult but still the biggest step to your freedom from debt.

We are all used to certain things that we are ready to defend and consider necessary in our lives. Such things give us some sort of release, and maybe an escape from our daily realities. I personally had a craving for gourmet meals. I love the appealing, fancy restaurants, and the allure of choice meals from choice menus, but I had to substitute those with equally amazing meals from my kitchen at home. In the process, I did save myself some much-needed money to settle debt. You may need to do a sincere roll call of your own life and identify key areas where you have money leaks, which in some instances can be channelled towards paying off some debt, no matter how little. It can range from unnecessary subscriptions to societal pressures of all sorts. I know of a number of gentlemen whose daily or weekly habits include having to go barhopping just to loosen up from financial pressure. But while their ties are loose for a drinking frenzy, debt, in many instances, is tightening its own noose even harder.

Is that holiday necessary? Is the fancy school for your kids, which you can't afford, necessary? Is that shiny electronic gadget upgrade necessary? Is that shiny car that attracts glances from neighbours and admiration from peers necessary? Are those fancy designer bags and jewellery necessary? Is your presence needed at every social shindig that requires a new outfit and shoes to match? Is that credit card that masquerades as a saviour really necessary? Is that new smart television necessary? Are those take-out meals every week necessary?

Many people are buying things they don't need to impress individuals who probably don't like them and whose opinions don't pay their bills. The best weight you will ever lose is not the calories, but people's opinions of you.

You must be honest with yourself about what a necessity is and what is an unnecessary want, and you must also have the sincere willingness to make lifestyle changes that will see you spend less than you earn. Your goal is to ensure income always tips the scale over outgoings, especially those greatly amplified by our shortsightedness and often not well-thought-through lifestyle choices.

You seek to be debt-free? Then you must change your lifestyle TODAY!

Remember, when in debt, you don't have to scratch every itch to spend. It will be unfair for anyone to make you disillusioned that this will be fun because it is not. Human beings are creatures of habit, and I bet you have a fixed way of doing things already. This will be adversely affected if what you truly want is debt freedom.

17. Income Increment

*"Now he who supplies seed to the sower
and bread for your food, and multiply your seed sown
and increase the fruits of your righteousness."*
- 2 Corinthians 9:10, KJV

True to its character, debt often leaves one disillusioned and properly beaten down. Unfortunately, this is not the time you should sit indoors with window blinds drawn and disheveled. Rather, it's the very time you need to be up and about. Many days, I also found solace in the darkness my room afforded. I shut out totally from the world, which I considered unfair to me, yet I was economical with the truth that I was deserving of where I was.

The stark realization you must embrace is the fact that the debt is waiting and often swells in size if ignored. You need to earn more because, like we already identified, you probably first got into debt because your income paled in significance to your spending habits. Therefore, the goal here is that you must increase your income or earnings; this should be enough motivation to get you off your backside to go out and get creative and productive.

There is a need for anyone in debt to draw from the inner recesses of their mind to create a spark that is needed to bring in more money. This is also another reason to buttress my earlier point on ego. I am a firm believer that everything you do to bring in income, as long as it is legal, is honorable. When in debt, one must adopt an eagle-like vision for jobs and opportunities that present themselves. Remember, you are a gazelle trying to escape; therefore, you must be ready to push your possibilities to the very precipice.

You can also liquidate assets you own that are not necessities to shore up your position and financial standing. Except for some heavenly intervention, or if you are willed a huge fortune by a long-forgotten relative, or if you win the national lottery, you would have to increase your income to supplement your necessary living expenses and also keep your creditors at bay. This is a strategic action you must take.

18. Don't Forget You Must Also Take Care of Your Needs

*"No one hates his own body but feeds
and cares for it, just as Christ cares for the Church."*
- Ephesians 5:29, NIV

One of the biggest mistakes most individuals in debt make is that, in a quest to rid themselves of the chains of debt, they forget that they still have a life to live and that only the living can offset debt. After all, a man who is six feet under the ground cannot service his debt and is of no use to a creditor or anyone else, for that matter. I recall a real-life story about a man who owed money to a creditor, who would visit him every Friday to demand payment. The debtor would plead for consideration and offer him an amount, but he rejected it. The creditor stormed out, promising a repeat visit on the preceding Monday. True to his word, he arrived at the residence to make good on his threat and met with an ongoing funeral, and upon further inquiry, he would discover the debtor had passed away that very weekend. He would go on to lament not taking the option given to him a few days ago, with little regard for the deceased.

Always ensure that you contribute a percentage of your income to not just exiting debt avenue, but do your best to meet up with paying your essential bills. After all, you don't want to be in debt and also homeless, without energy or water, or even unable to feed yourself and your family. Also, while this may sound self-serving, it's a necessary path to take, especially if your intention is to pay off your debt and have a life to live afterwards. So, the rule of thumb is to fix a percentage of whatever comes in and take care of your personal needs, not only your obligation to creditors who would continue living long after the individual is on the streets, declared bankrupt, or, in the worst case, in a grave.

19. Honesty

"Whoever walks in integrity walks securely,
but whoever takes crooked paths will be found out."
- Proverbs 10:9, NIV

Many individuals are wearing masks, which is why there is an African adage that says the clothes on a person are hiding a lot of things. A strategic action you must take is to be honest with everyone, especially those closest to you. It is bad enough that you are in debt; it's a mess, and of what use is the mask to hide you away? You want to get out of this soonest, and you will, but only if you come out clean to everyone by taking off the mask.

For years, I had mine on, and it was a charade. The honesty I advocate will likely spur much-needed support, sympathy, and so much more. It will also create the opportunity and platform you need to approach creditors with clean hands. Like I earlier highlighted, debt is not a life sentence, and you can still go on to have an amazing life (if anything would encourage you, it is the fact that success always wipes away past failures, and human beings are naturally fickle and seemingly endowed with short memories once you climb back up).

You must decide to be honest with everyone—no half-truths or half-lies—and set out to be free from deceit and untruthfulness. You owe everyone the truth—family, professionals, creditors, yourself, and God. You will then truly discover that the truth indeed sets free; it is a key that opens the padlocks on the iron bars of debt prison.

Proverbs 12:19 (NIV) says,

> *"Truthful lips endure forever,*
> *but a lying tongue lasts only a moment."*

You want to choose freedom over bondage? Then you must embrace honesty when you are on the quest to cut off the past and create a new future that is void of the avoidable mistakes, errors, and heartaches that accompany debt. Do not carry on living a pretentious life like everything is fine when you are in trouble; don't be that duck gliding seemingly smooth in the pond while underneath is paddling furiously. You must rid yourself of the temptation of playing in the gallery to save face; you simply cannot give what you do not have. Take a few steps back and assess your position, then move ahead with honesty.

The day I embraced this principle, despite the overwhelming and crippling fear that held my confidence in a chokehold, was my own day of liberation that inevitably kicked in motion a series of events that would see me become debt-free. You too can do the same and share the wonderful results I did.

20. Communication

"Let your conversations be always
full of grace, seasoned with salt so you may know
how to answer everyone?"
– *Colossians 4:6, NIV*

I once had an employee who struggled with communication when under pressure from another party. I came to understand that it was his nature and his in-built defence mechanism. He would switch off his phones, ignore messages, etc. All of which were frustrating for us, his colleagues, but that's exactly how many of us handle creditors when in debt. We choose to ignore calls and messages, further infuriating them to take drastic actions against us.

A very strategic step is to ensure that the communication lines remain open. The least you owe the creditor is an update on the efforts being undertaken to pay off the debt. Sometimes the feedback may not be what they want to hear, but keeping them in the loop about things on your end is by far more honourable than going incommunicado on them. Sometimes I must admit it could be choking; this I know. At times, I felt like smashing my phone against a wall, and after a call, I would feel so physically exhausted that I would collapse in a confused heap, tears of uncertainty streaming down my cheeks. During those emotionally draining moments, further communication was the least on my agenda. My mental health was suffering from the barrage of abuses, insults, and threats.

So, I had to come up with a balance. And honestly, in order to think constructively about how to dig myself out of this debt hole, I needed my mind working at top capacity. I would have to take what I called a quick mind holiday that necessitated me switching off communication for a brief period, but not to fall short of my own rule. I would inform the creditors of my being inaccessible for a period and would be prompt in responding to text messages, WhatsApp messages, and emails that I may have missed during the interlude. Communication is a key strategy that should be employed.

21. Your Mind and Staying Positive

"Finally, brethren, whatsoever things are true,
whatsoever things are honest, whatsoever things are just,
whatsoever things are pure, whatsoever things are lovely,
whatsoever things are of good report; if there be any virtue,
and if there be any praise, think on these things."
- Philippians 4:8, NIV

You are mandated to guard your peace; no one is going to do this for you. In the earlier example given, I would maximize the interlude periods and sleep—yes, just sleep. I would give my body a chance at recovery. I knew full well that a few hours of good sleep would not only energize my mind but also ensure I stayed positive to face whatever was to come.

Many in debt make the mistake of allowing their minds to stay clouded through the 24 hours of the day with so much negativity, thereby sometimes causing irreparable damage to their minds and bodies. I personally know the power of sound to influence moods. So, I would surround myself with soul-lifting music. I would put a number of my favourite gospel tracks on repeat and have visual images surround me that trigger my mind positively. At that point, my mind released the much-needed creative juices and fuel to propel me forward.

Recall that relaxation increases blood flow throughout our bodies, allowing us to utilize more energy effectively. Another major advantage is that we tend to have a much calmer and clearer mind, which in turn aids positive thinking, concentration, memory, and decision-making. Your mind and body in a relaxed state will slow your heart rate, reduce high blood pressure, which is often a byproduct of overthinking about debt, and help relive tensions. Therefore, it is instructive that you don't let debt steal your peace. Stay positive and keep your mind at an optimal level to work for your benefit and become debt-free.

Occasionally, please give yourself a treat and take yourself out. You don't have to feel guilty, as long as it is not overboard and a further drain on your resources. I had a few escape places; one was an affordable little restaurant by the Lagos lagoon. I was always empty during the day, and it afforded me the tranquilly and silence to think, strategize, and most importantly, pray. It was a huge psychological boost that did wonders for my already charged mind, or it was indulging in my favourite gelato ice cream treat—your choice.

22. Take Charge of Those Emotions

"Do not be anxious about anything, but in everything by prayer and supplication with thanksgiving let your request be made known to God."
- Philippians 4:6, NIV

Emotions are powerful. They are neutral, like fire, and capable of both construction and destruction. Therefore, one has to learn to master them to make the most of them. Emotions can be triggered by individuals, events, and circumstances.

There were times I was unsure of exactly what I was feeling. I felt like a human cocktail, and at every instance, there was a little bit of anxiety, a splash of frustration, a drop of regret, two teaspoons of stress, half a glass of loneliness, two ounces of shame, and a huge sprinkle of sadness to taste, etc. And it can sometimes be too much for one sane person to handle, but you can.

The action I took was to first label the various emotions, thereby disempowering them over me; it was what you identify that you can go on to conquer. I took the firm decision that I was no longer going to be a bouncing ball, unsure of how high or low I would be thrown by my creditors. If you want to get out of debt, you must take back control of your emotions by being responsible for your response.

In my book, Get Ahead: Practical Steps to Life's Realities and Embrace Success, I identified a formula that has worked for me (which I picked up from Stephen R. Covey's groundbreaking book, 7 Habits of Highly Effective People). I have advocated for thousands of individuals who I have had the opportunity to teach and mentor, which is:

$$E \text{ (Event)} + R(\text{Response}) = O(\text{Outcome})$$

The event is a certainty: you would have sharp arrows fired at you, and due to your disadvantageous position, you may not have the luxury of putting up a shield or a block. Therefore, your response is the only variable you control. The importance of this fact cannot be overemphasized as it determines the final outcome you face on your debt journey. The ability to embrace this would clearly allow you to be conscious of your ability to control the narrative of the emotions that seek to overwhelm you. Remember, like most things in life, it's all down to a choice. Also, it is important to have knowledge of your emotional triggers so as to create a defence mechanism to overcome them, because for a certain time, when in debt, they will come.

23. Health

"Do you not know that your bodies are temples
of the Holy Spirit who is in you, whom you have
received from God? You are not your own."
- 1 Corinthians 6:19, NIV

'Health is wealth' is a well-known saying that means a state of well-being—free from diseases, both physical and mental. It is taken from the writings of a great classical Roman Poet, Virgil's "Publius Vergilius Maro," popular for saying,

"The greatest wealth is health."

Many times, people have suffered bad health, me included, due to the psychological breakdown resulting from debt. Early on, I said that when I was in debt, I felt like I was in a boxing bout with debt with my hands tied behind me. This gave my opponent (debt) the unchecked liberty to pound me to its heart's content. With loud screams and cheers coming from the crowd who enjoyed a good fight and were convinced that the canvas of the financial boxing ring was my end.

When in debt, you must be conscious of your health. Listen to your body. Watch out for changing signs and out-of-character signals. This is so important and cannot be overemphasized. Many have died from a myriad of ailments brought on by debt. I have heard tales of people who suffered strokes and were not even aware. I remember occasions when food was not a priority for me and I would go on long periods without eating—on unwitting hunger strikes of sorts—and I would need to be reminded to eat. By so doing, I was robbing my body of much-needed nutrition and vitamins, thus sentencing myself to seasons of sickness that went on to deplete my already severely damaged financial position.

The importance of being strategic and acknowledging that health is wealth cannot be overemphasized. You must make up your mind first to stay alive. Secondly, to ensure that your life is free from sickness and diseases, the best assistance you can offer the human body is nutrition. You could use a lot of rest and nutritious food. You must take responsibility for your own health, irrespective of the financial pressures chiming in your ears. Again, I put it to you that only the healthy and living can offset debt.

24. Support System

"When there is no guidance, a people fall,
but in an abundance of counselors there is safety."
- Proverbs 11:14, ESV

You have to identify and embrace the importance of a beneficial and positive support system. Identifying and building one that will help you through a trying season is truly a blessing. It takes wisdom to recognize this and run with it. You must acknowledge the role of guidance and be thankful for those who stand with you during those times, because in their counsel you will find safety.

I went on holiday once to the beautiful island of Zanzibar with my wife, and we were encouraged to go kayaking. At the time, my wife could not swim, while I could swim pretty well. One of the instructions handed to us by the instructor manning one of those yellow banana-shaped canoes you find at resorts was that if we both paddled in unison, we would both travel fairly easily. A funny incident would happen during the short ride: I would have a nasty muscle cramp that would make what was a fun outing a very painful adventure while we were still in the middle of the water. I obviously could no longer paddle, so my wife had to do all the paddling by herself. She literally became my lifesaver and support system. It's similar to my debt experience; I needed my spouse to ride along with other key individuals to guide and help me paddle my life's boat back to shore from a position where debt had kept me anchored to one spot in pain and hopelessly left me immobilized.

You should identify and befriend those who will be your useful companions and also give you helpful counsel. When in debt, your decision-making is often suspect due to so much going on around you, and it is important that it be X-rayed by those who are not swamped by emotions and can give logical counsel to see you through.

25. Self-Financial Date

*"Know the state of your flocks, and put your
heart into caring for your herds. For riches don't last
forever and the crown might not be passed to
the next generation. After the hay is harvested
and the new crop appears and the mountain grasses
are gathered in, your sheep will provide wool
for clothing, and your goats will provide the price
of a field. And you will have enough goat's milk f
or yourself, your family and your servant girls."*
– Proverbs 27:23–27, NIV

Be intentional about knowing the state of your financial affairs (flocks). I faltered here. I was oblivious to the state of my flocks, and clearly, I could not get any ROI from them due to my negligence. A very strategic move is to organize a weekly or monthly money date with yourself and the Holy Spirit to review your financial position. There is no flight without a leap. In your financial planning, let God be your financial advisor, budget manager, accounts representative, and auditor.

Remember, we have highlighted how individuals get into debt, and one of them is burying their heads in the sand like ostriches. The opposite is now required to escape debt, which is for you to bring your head out and face head-on the financial issues plaguing your life.

Pick a convenient time that works for you when you can have a self-date to be true and sincere with yourself. This exercise will help you pinpoint areas where your attention must be focused. This would guarantee that you channel your efforts towards the critical areas that require it.

This could be daily, weekly, monthly, or quarterly (longer periods could work when you are debt-free). I mostly had to take daily glances at my positions or every other few days to ascertain my financial reality. This is one strategic move you cannot in any way ignore. If you ignore it, it's at your own peril.

If this is a struggle for you, as a matter of necessity, identify an individual with sufficient financial knowledge who can help review your financial status, give a sound analysis of your position, and offer advisory services on how you can be not only debt-free but also financially buoyant. This date is a no-holds-barred, realistic, and brutal assessment of where you are financially and what needs to be corrected for you and your finances to be better.

CHAPTER 6

HOW IS DEBT PAID OFF?

You must understand that my personal stance on paying off debt is from a personal, scriptural, ethical, and integrity standpoint, which is premised on the belief that all debt must be paid. It doesn't matter how long; don't just wish it away. Debt repayment reveals your character much more than anything else; it reestablishes trust.

Little wonder why Psalm 37:21 (NIV) says, "the wicked borrow and do not repay." It categorizes those who lack the intent to pay as wicked. And if you are gunning for heavenly things, there's breaking news for you located in Luke 16:11 (NLT),

> *"And if you are untrustworthy about worldly wealth, who will trust you with the true riches of heaven?'*

This clearly indicates that your accountability to resources starts while you are still here on earth, not only when you get to heaven.

What, therefore, are the ways by which debt is paid off? They include the following:

1. Divine Providence

"The Silver is mine, and the gold is mine,
says the Lord of Heaven's Armies."
- Haggai 2:8, NIV

I am 100% unapologetic about reiterating the role of the Almighty God in helping those who seek His face when in dire situations concerning debt. While this may not be the modus operandi of how He operates when it comes to our finances, it is nevertheless one of the ways, through faith in Him, that payments of debts can be made. He can, in His mercy, make an exception to the general rule.

It is really clear when one digs deeper into the biblical story of Jesus and the fish with the coin. For better perspective, try to picture a fish with a coin in its mouth. It was evident that He pulled off a miracle for the ages to try and avoid offense. Matthew 17:27 says expressly, *"but so that we do not offend them."* Clearly debt attracts offense, and Jesus underscored the importance of paying His temple tax or tribute money.

One of the greatest revelations I received was that of

seed faith, from one of our departed fathers of faith, Oral Roberts. The illumination I was exposed to was an infallible reality: that one must learn to plant a seed of equivalent benefit to take hold of the loss in defeat, failure, etc. If you are in debt, you can equally sow seed in faith, look to God to grow the seed, and trust Him as a source. Expect a miracle harvest and see what God will do despite the situation and storms of life saying otherwise. James 2:20 clearly lets us know that faith without works is dead. Therefore, it is the fertilizer that your seed needs to yield increase.

I saw this happen severally in my debt situation, wherein from unexpected sources, I would receive resources I did not even imagine possible. Especially from individuals that I least expected and that I think is the whole point—things happening for our good without an ounce of input from us. Sometimes it was not financial but in the currency of human relationships, all lined up like dominoes to see me escape the grueling cycles of debt.

Remember the widow we spoke about earlier in our discourse? The one who approached Elisha on the day the devil intended to be her worst, and God turned it into her best day. Not only was there a miracle, but it also birthed a surplus that was beyond her wildest dream. "She went and told the man of God, and he said, "Go, sell the oil and pay your debts. You and your sons can live on what is left" (2 Kings 4:7). God's intervention through his prophet was so spectacular that it was obvious it was an exception to the general rule. That same God is still actively in the business of breaking protocols in righteousness and takes no days off.

2. Debt Forgiveness, Mercy, and Cancellations

"The earth is the Lord's and everything in it.
The world and all its people belong to Him."
- Psalm 24:1, NIV

First, you should know that our God is a debt-cancelling God. He is no respecter of man and He wants you debt-free. Going through Scripture, we read more about the cancellation of debts than many other miracles.

I remember quite vividly going to a creditor's office, pretty much unsure of the reception I would get. I just woke up, put a call across, and requested a meeting to discuss my debt. When seated in his office, I watched him get busy on the phones. With bated breath, I rehearsed in my head how to request more time to pay off my debt. I had hardly spoken a few sentences when the gentleman would immediately utter words that would leave me in tears. "You don't have to owe me anymore; I have written off the debt," were the words which gently left his lips and alighted on my soul like the first rain on a desert. What I owed this gentleman ran into millions. He simply just deleted it all to my utter amazement.

I was still gob-smacked when he explained how he was a product of mercy and had to extend the same to me. I came to the realization that mercy was real, and I have been its consistent beneficiary on several occasions. My prayer for you is that God's mercy triumph in your case, give you beauty in the place of mourning, and the garment of praise in the place of sorrow.

In 2 Kings 6:6-7, the story of the borrowed axe also highlights God's mercy. A young man borrowed an axe, and while cutting down trees, the head fell into the river, and his desperate cry reveals the burden of debt "… Alas master for it was borrowed". A cry of desperation moved the prophet to cause the axe head to miraculously swim to the surface, and he put out his hand and took it (an average weight of 2.5 lb. of metal floating to the surface must have been a spectacle).

You can seek the mercy of God, and even your creditors can bless you when you are underserving. Debt is like a wrecking ball, and you need divine strength to stop its deleterious impact, and only mercy possesses such push-back capacity.

A caveat I must add is: you must also remember to extend mercy to others, just as you enjoy mercy yourself. So, from now and when you get out of debt, show the same or a higher level of understanding to others who will be at your mercy. This is very important because Jesus Himself said, blessed are the merciful, for they shall obtain mercy (Matthew 5:7).

Matthew 18:23-34 (NIV), paints a masterpiece to buttress this point:

> *"Therefore, the kingdom of Heaven*
> *can be compared to a king who decided to*
> *bring his accounts up to date with servants who*
> *had borrowed money from him. In the process,*
> *one of his debtors was brought in who owed him*
> *millions of dollars. He couldn't pay so his master*
> *ordered that he be sold-along with his wife,*
> *his children, and everything he owned—to pay*
> *the debt. But the man fell down before his master*
> *and begged him, "Please be patient*
> *with me, and I will pay it all."*

Then his master was filled with pity got him, and he released him and forgave his debt. "But when the man left the king, he went to a fellow servant who owed him a few thousand dollars. He grabbed him by the throat and demanded instant payment. His fellow servant fell down before him and begged him for a little more time. "Be patient with me, and I will pay it; he pleaded. But his creditor wouldn't wait. He had the man arrested and put in prison until the debt could be paid in full.

When some of the other servants saw this, they were very upset. They went to the King and told him everything that had happened. Then the King called in the man he had forgiven and said, 'You evil servant! I forgave you that tremendous debt because you pleaded with me. Shouldn't you have mercy on your fellow servant, just as I had mercy on you?'

Then the angry king sent the man to prison to be tortured until he had paid his entire debt."

It goes without saying that God can do anything, including debt cancellation.

Jeremiah 32:17 (NKJV) testifies,

*"Ah, Lord God! Behold you have
made the heavens and the earth by your
great power and outstretched arm. There is
nothing too hard for you."*

The miracle of debt cancellation is only a reality with heavenly intervention. Hardly would you find a lender in their right mind who would want to release you from your debt obligation to them. Definitely not! With their own worries, needs, and concerns pressing hard against them on all sides.

A friend shared the story of a debtor who owed a military

officer a huge sum. He was given a deadline, at which point the creditor was going to use the full weight of his office to inflict severe punishment for defaulting. In desperation and with less than twenty-four hours to go, after staring at the ground, he decided to change his view to the heavens. The story goes that the next morning, the creditor, in a state of apprehension, told him his debt was forgiven. What happened was only divinely orchestrated. The creditor had what I would term a night to forget (for similar reference, remember the unnamed wife of Pontius Pilate to understand better). Now, while I advocate for you to be honorable enough to pay off your debt obligations, there would be debts that could be cancelled if it were the will of God. In Proverbs 21:1 (KJV), Scripture says,

> *"The king's heart is in the hand of the Lord,*
> *as the rivers of water: he turneth it*
> *whithersoever He will".*

> *"Share each other's burdens,*
> *and in this way obey the law of Christ"*
> *- Galatians 6:2, NIV*

If you are blessed with this avenue, you will soon realize that helpers will play a major role in the extirpation of your debt. You are one blessed individual to have another fellow human being inconvenience themselves to see you untangled from debt. Like I have stressed before, the rule is for you to come clean. I enjoyed this significantly, and I had a spouse, parents, siblings, and a few good friends providing help to pay off a percentage of my own personal debt portfolio after coming clean. Though it appeared like I was going to be crucified, I ended up receiving overwhelming financial help to settle pressing needs and the creditors, and you can as well.

A major debt repayment mechanism is reaching out to those who can help and support you, but remember what I said earlier: no one owes you anything! Be grateful for whatever you get. It is a very viable option, as it will come to you out of love, goodwill, and with no strings attached. Mostly, you don't have to live with the stigma of hanging interests and crushing debt. What I received was more of encouragement, prayers, knowledge, counsel, etc., not finance.

To make the most of this, you must set aside shyness, shame, ego, and seek support. You must also be discerning in your requests so as to channel them to those with the capacity to help. In my case, I chose not to underestimate or overestimate anyone. People will come into and go out of your life. Stay discerning and strategic in your requests. Some people open the doors to their own freedom through an act of kindness towards others. Remember the widow at Zarephath who encountered Elijah?

Finally, if you have a helper like the Prophet Elijah, sometimes all you need is capacity, that is, many empty containers to contain the overflow.

3. Create a Deliberate and Systematic Repayment Plan

"Give to everyone what you owe them: pay your taxes
and government fees to those who collect them, and give
respect and honor to those who are in authority."
– Romans 13:7, NIV

If you are to overcome the spirit of debt, you must have a powerful plan that uses the very force of God to guarantee your victory.

Earlier, I identified the role of professionals such as lawyers, financial planners, and debt mediators. Or maybe you can find a friendly hand who can help create a payment plan tied to your income and not just probabilities. This is particularly applicable if you have a job or a source of livelihood.

A debt-free plan is the one strategy that must be created, because repaying your debt honors God and is the right legal thing to do. So how do you intend to pay? Who do you intend to pay first? When you get an income? You must not leave anything to chance, as every dime you earn in this season is useful. Therefore, you must create a deliberate and systematic repayment plan which will be communicated to creditors to guarantee a way out.

My family members, in some instances, alongside the above-mentioned professionals, helped me put across those very uncomfortable calls. They attended negotiation meetings and became important intermediaries to ensure a set and functional plan, where possible, was in place.

This guaranteed me the much-needed clarity and time to run around and keep to my obligations. It also helped creditors plan accordingly and gave them hope that their money wouldn't be lost due to errors or otherwise. Many times, such arrangements were instrumental in warding off any potential shame or disgrace that could be looming.

Remember, you never want to push anyone to the wall, where they feel that they have nothing to lose and are ready to drag you all the way to the gallows. It's a road you must be determined never to get on and one of the most viable ways to achieving this is by entering into an agreement with all those you owe. This, of course, should be based on a sincere assessment of your circumstances to pay off the debt.

So, get to work and create a repayment plan that will see you become debt-free and ensure that terms of settlement are executed by both parties.

4. Liquidation of Assets

More often than not, you may be forced to liquidate assets, which would aid you in your debt repayment. You would have to take stock of what you own and weigh what you truly need and can let go of. Some of the item may have strong sentimental value, but the sale of precious items can generate quick and significant income to pay off debt. This may be cars, lands, securities, clothing, jewelry, etc. It is better to rid yourself of debt by temporarily ridding yourself of your so-called valuables than to remain in debt in the unnecessary company of your valuables.

The items you 'lose' today, you can choose to replace when you become debt-free tomorrow. There is no point looking rich when hounded by creditors, so you must do your own garage sale to guarantee a much-needed liquidation to be truly debt-free.

Many are in debt and are, in some cases by things that can pay off their debts or put them back on the road to recovery. How many cars do you need? Are those fancy mobile phones really necessary? What are you still doing with those jewelry and art pieces? Why are you still nurturing those properties? Why should you continue eating out at those expensive restaurants? What are you still doing with the expensive furniture? Why are there still six cars in your garage?

In my case, I was in a position to sell off real estate to start paying off huge amounts. Ask anyone who has ever tasted debt; they will tell you how much they would rather be debt-free and eating instant noodles than be surrounded by the appearance of opulence and be constantly hounded by this relentless beast called debt.

5. Creation of Multiple Income Streams

"A river flowed from the land of Eden, watering the garden and then dividing into four branches."
– Genesis 2:10, NIV

A major debt repayment strategy that I explored entails the creation of multiple income streams. We have earlier established that sometimes the inability to match income with outgoings could lead to debt. Now that you have found yourself in debt, the very thing that would have kept you debt-free in the first place is what must be explored to get you out of the red. You have to go beyond your established comfort levels, whether this involves taking one or more jobs (in a post-COVID world, there are now more global remote job opportunities available to seekers).

Any way you can increase your income legally is highly welcome. At this level, I would say you must extinguish every form, color and level of pride. As long as it brings income, using the famous Nike slogan, *"Just do it."*

When it comes to paying off the premium embarrassment called debt, nothing is too embarrassing or beneath you. You must consciously launch yourself into a state of mind to explore strategies that would bring in money. Which weekend gigs are available? What freelance activities can you take up? It's limitless if you put your mind to becoming a multiple-earner. The possibility of extinguishing debt through one income stream is extremely difficult to achieve.

The same energy it takes to borrow is the same energy it takes to be creative to earn an income. So, it's time for you to harness your creativity to improve your financial position. To be fully debt-free would mean having to start new things and discarding some old ones. You would have to do what people who are in a debt mess should do: take action. Inaction sponsors your continuous stay in the grip of debt. So, you must make an attempt to just do something profitable. Not everything may work, but you are more likely to pull out a winning card from the deck when you are playing at the table.

James 1:22 (KJV), says,

*"...be ye doers of the word and
not hearers only, deceiving your own selves."*

6. Use Your God-given Skills and Abilities

*"Every good gift and every perfect gift
is from above, and cometh down from the
father of lights, with whom is no variableness,
neither shadow of turning."*
– James 1:7, KJV

Everyone is blessed with a God-given, inherent skill and ability that would create and attract value. The indisputable fact is that money flows toward value. So, there is a need to push out the unique proposition you possess to the world. During my debt journey, I had to closely identify the skills and abilities that could be monetized. I was a natural communicator/ trainer and felt I was a good writer. So, I put these skills to use, pushing out books that did not require any additional qualification or endorsement by a third party. I became an overnight salesman, pushing out copies of my materials.

On some occasions I had no choice than to subsidize my training and speaking fees to individuals and organizations just to ensure income did come in. I took up online mentoring jobs, and I would split up the sums from my earnings and whatever substantial amount was left went straight to debt liquidation.

So what skills do you possess? You may be surprised by what the Almighty has endued you with that could attract the value you need to be debt-free. Skills and abilities would by their nature, in most instances, deliver value if properly harnessed and dispensed. When you are conscious of them, and you refine and package them to the point people find them helpful and useful, money would definitely flow your way.

Typing right now on my laptop, a few feet away is my son's tutor, Miss Glory, whose skill and ability is teaching toddlers (something that is surely not easy). She teaches a number of children in my community, and in the process, attracts more income with her skills and ability. Again, remember the widow that Elijah prayed for? It is very instructive to know that God will provide the oil if we get the jars. So, get as many jars as possible to be filled. Do not limit yourself like in the story, when the oil ceased because there was no more vessel to hold it.

CHAPTER 7

HOW TO AVOID REPEATED CYCLES OF DEBT

*"And now dear brothers and sisters,
one final thing. Fix your thoughts on what
is true, and honorable, and right, and pure,
and lovely, and admirable. Think about things
that are excellent and worthy of praise."*

(Philippians 4:8, NLT)

I would be doing you, the reader, great injustice if I stopped at the previous chapter and ended this book there. If I do not progress to warn you that you can become debt-free, offer prayers to the heavens, make promises to yourself, declare vows to your loved ones, and still find yourself relapse into the same mess. How do I know this? Well, I ended up back at square one again.

There is no scientific proof for the correlation between birds and animals before rainfall or natural disasters. But more often than not, we can almost all agree that animals seem to have some sort of heightened senses at the earliest sign of trouble (at least our domestic pets at home prove this over and over again). It's that same heightened reaction you must develop—the sixth sense that runs off at the slightest sign of debt. Because your inability to ignore this friendly advice will lead to the possibility of you repeating your debt class again, just like I did. The goal of this book is to get you debt-free and ensure you never have to relive the nightmare ever again.

You must become your own financial doctor by ensuring you diagnose your own peculiar debt root cause with the mission to ensure that the tree will never grow again. At the second instance, many people are more unforgiving and less understanding, believing you must have learnt your lessons during the first episode. But not everyone is that magnanimous in their love and understanding. You cannot afford to leave the roots of debt in the ground; everything must be uprooted.

I discovered sometimes that when debt is paid, there seems to be the presence of what is described in medicine as phantom pain—this pain feels like it's coming from a body part that is no longer there, similar to what an amputee feels. There were periods when I felt that debt was still present, and this was purely a psychological warfare to overcome and convince yourself of its departure. Another analogy that reveals the depth of the debt battle is when you liken it to the battle of an alcoholic who is capable of having relapses despite initial victories.

It is the reason the AA (Alcohol Anonymous) would borrow us a principle to avoid a relapse into debt, and that is, "the only path to victory over the battle is to make no exceptions." If you interview members of the AA, you would be regaled with tales of woes on how the first drink after the last proved to be their downfall, and they wound up on the skid row again.

This is no different than an individual who is used to debt and sees it as the first point of consideration when making decisions. It is for this reason that guard rails are needed to prevent individuals from falling overboard. Debt is an affliction that you must never allow to arise a second time. Once you taste it again, its magnetic powers almost guarantee you don't stop until you become enslaved again.

How then do we fight the battle and stop ourselves from returning to the trenches of the debt warfare?

1. Discipline

"No discipline is enjoyable while it is
happening—it's painful! But afterward
there will be a peaceful harvest of right living
for those who trained in this way."
- Hebrews 12:11, NIV

Discipline is training and developing through instruction, and building self-control.

Imbibing some needed discipline to avoid sinking back into debt due to the scars I had borne was hard. I had to make some decisions and stick to them. Some were what you may consider little, and others, major. I would discipline myself from borrowing airtime on my mobile phone, something most mobile telecommunications operators offered cheaply, because I understood that very little habits aggregate to become mountains of character.

So, you must equally identify areas in your life where you must make up your mind. So, you must equally identify areas in your life where you must make up your mind, like when you decide on weight loss or receive a life-threating prognosis from a doctor on the need for a lifestyle change that would require discipline to survive. It's the same wavelength; it's all about discipline.

Discipline is the glue that holds all the pieces of your life together for progress and advancement. Without which, what would become of your life would be chaotic disorder.

2. Contentment

"But godliness with contentment is great gain."
– 1 Timothy 6:6

We live in a consumption-driven world where there is a monstrous urge to keep consuming, amassing, and increasing. While there is nothing wrong with ambition or increase, many have found themselves in repeated cycles of debt due their inability to draw a line in the sand.

Indeed, when you are content, you suppress the inordinate urges that lead to debt. Any individual that is able to attain the height of contentment is one that will always be head above the stormy waters of debt. It is a height that guarantees financial serenity and peace throughout your life. Do not be swept away by man-made systems and structures that perpetuate an endless desire of expansion without moderation. Even the most expensive car is useless without brakes.

Contentment puts a leash, lid, and barricade on any form of excess. It keeps one grounded in the needful and cuts off the frivolous. There is wisdom in contentment whose walls resist the visit of debt.

It is indeed "better to have little, with fear for the Lord, than to have great treasure and inner turmoil" (Proverbs 15:16, NLT).

3. Install Financial Alarm Bells

*"A man without self-control is like a city
broken into and left without walls."*
- Proverbs 25:28

Alarm bells are warning systems built to inform us when trouble is approaching or nearby. Therefore, another major target to keep you from a relapse is to create alarm bells when you see yourself slipping down the rabbit hole of debt.

Homes, vehicles, and offices should not be the only things guarded by alarm systems. Your financial systems must be well-guarded against excesses. Whether it is cutting up your credit cards, one debt advisor described it as "plastic surgery," putting daily spending limits to whatever that will stop you.

In some cases, individuals have been known to have daily spending limits or even to link bank account alerts to their accountability partners to ensure they don't go overboard and help measure if their intended purchase is necessary. Firm decisions must be put in place that will show all parties when financial trouble is looming like doom which is usually preceded by a period of financial recklessness. You will have to give up some of your financial liberty, but it is a price worth paying.

4. Reduce Liabilities

"And having food and raiment
let us be therewith content."
- 1 Timothy 6:8, KJV

It is vital that you reduce expenses and get used to being content with less. Whatever you do with your little income is probably a reflection of the pattern that will be in force when your income increases.

I found myself back in the whirlwind of debt, unsure of how I failed to be free despite my previous debt experience. Upon honest assessment, I found out I had ignored reducing my liabilities. Instead, despite my lower income, I increased liabilities that led me to more debt.

A culture of unchecked consumption won't help you by any twist or stretch of happenstance. Thus, you must sit down, identify the liabilities you have, and make a conscious decision to increase your assets. Assets are identified as an item of property owned by a person or company, regarded as having value, and available to meet debts, commitments, or legacies. It is therefore not an option if you seek true financial prosperity. As the above definition highlights, one of the things it guards you against is debt.

5. Keep Fleeing from All Appearances of Debt

"Stay away from every kind of evil."
- 1 Thessalonians 5:22, NIV

I recognize that the Bible does not expressly call debt a

sin, but it does equate it to bondage and likens it to a curse—two unpalatable circumstances for any individual to find themselves under. We earlier pointed out the need to flee, but this is not a one-time action. To avoid a repeat, it is almost a daily routine that must be inculcated into your thinking until it becomes second nature to you every time you are triggered by anything or anyone that could lead you to debt. You must remember the pain, the shame, and the embarrassment and flee.

I personally retain some painful and harsh reminders of that season that are enough to cause me to flee from every appearance of debt. So, this may be an old letter from a creditor or anything else that is enough to get your mind racing.

6. Accountability Partners

"As iron sharpens iron,
so a friend sharpens a friend."
- Proverbs 27:17, NIV

One of the most important guard rails I had to install that ended repeated cycles was the presence of an accountability partner, and in my case, the obvious choice was my wife. I had to shed the societally conditioned alpha male mindset I had carried for years, ignoring my covenant companion.

Financial struggles and stress are no good boosters for any marriage. It is important to have a common front and ensure decisions are jointly made. I had to become one with my spouse. A sincere appeal for help with accountability could keep you from returning to debt. An accountability partner would help you control habits that fuel debt, and help with income allocations, considering the fact that debt often finds its strength in the dark. When known only to the debtor, such individuals will ensure nothing stays hidden and your financial actions are screened to avoid the repeat of another unfortunate episode of debt.

7. Budgeting

"Good planning and hard work, lead to prosperity,
but hasty shortcuts lead to poverty."
- Proverbs 21:5, NIV

The need for budgeting is one that cannot be overemphasized. Nothing will rein in impulse spending and financial frivolity more than a budget. A budget will ensure you don't become indebted again, as it will help you allocate resources to essential needs, ensure savings, and make life truly worth living in peace and not confronted with constant worry.

While I admit that only a small percentage of individuals have the luxury of their income possessing the capacity to counter every bill that comes knocking, budgeting will bring about prudence and discipline that will see that you have your head above financial waters. Budgeting will ensure that you spend only what you have on what you need. And like I have often observed from my personal experience, time reveals the true value of things you buy. Remember, if you reject discipline, you only harm yourself.

Pliny the Elder, the Roman philosopher, once remarked that "an object in possession seldom retains the same charm it had in its pursuit." If you want to stay out of debt, you must become good friends with a budget. There are tons of budget samples online that you can edit and adopt. Thousands of budget apps and tools are available as well. Remember Luke 14:28 (NLT), *"But you don't begin until you count the cost. For who would begin construction of a building without first calculating the cost to see if there is enough money to finish it"*. Unfortunately, this was the foolishness driving the vehicle of my finances. I embarked on business ventures, and personal escapades without taking stock. I would find myself in the middle of the whirling sea with nothing more than an inflatable boat. The result was always capsizing into the murky waters of debt. You don't want to return to debt? Then get a budget to guide your finances.

8. Consciousness of External Triggers

"He who is impulsive exalts folly."
- Proverbs 14:29, NIV

In my case, I have often seen that modern-day media in every format is formed and crafted with a mandate to get you to act in a particular way— what is usually called programming. Often times, this programming is unfortunately not to your benefit.

We live in an age where interconnectivity between men and the publicity of their fellow humans and products is unprecedented in the history of mankind. There is a constant barrage of what is expected of you to keep buying, whether you need it or not. What this does is keep you in constant desire to acquire and, most likely, push you off the ledge into debt eventually. You must look out for external triggers that have been strategically placed around your life to ensure you remain in financial doldrums. So, you must be on guard at all times not to fall victim to an orchestrated campaign to get you to spend repeatedly, and end up in debt again.

9. Start Saving

"The wise store up choice food and olive oil,
but fools gulp theirs down."
– Proverbs 21:20, NIV

Is it not amazing that of all the creatures walking on God's green earth, His wisdom, which was expressed through King Solomon to make man understand the importance of saving, was interpreted through an ant? In Proverbs 6:6-8 (NIV), we all receive what I term a clear challenge,

Go to the ant, you sluggard; consider its ways and be wise! It has no commander, no overseer or ruler, yet it stores its provisions in summer and gathers its food at harvest.

I can tell you that savings is not easy; in fact, it's a very painful undertaking, just to say it like it is. You must be very gentle on yourself, make sure you create realistic targets, and pace yourself when you are on your savings journey. Once you get past the initial threshold of pain, you must understand that temptations will arise to return you to the past. Your responsibility is to ensure saving becomes a real habit.

Occasionally, I suffered what I may classify as withdrawal symptoms, but when it becomes a way of life, it becomes an automatic behavior that will serve you well going into the future and keep you from slipping back into the mud of debt. The culture of saving is something that must become the norm, considering the fact that in the life of almost every man there will be plenty of lean years. Just like in the times of Joseph, his hands-on wisdom pointed at savings as being the only action to guarantee the entire future of the then global superpower, Egypt!

10. Investments

*"Send your grain across the seas, and in time,
profits will flow back to you. But divide your
investments among many places, for you do not
know what risks might lie ahead."*
- Ecclesiastes 11:1–2, NIV

Once you become debt-free, it is essential that you put in place an investment plan. There is no one who stays out of debt and grows wealth without an investment of some sort. You must get professional assistance on investments, which will be based primarily on your risk levels. The necessity of a growing safety pot will guarantee a financially secure future and save you from exploring riskier options such as debt.

In today's world, the options are limitless, and the rewards are mostly tied to the risks taken. Investments are hardly risk-free, but still, that shouldn't scare you off to bury your money in the ground or, in my opinion, in a savings account attracting negligible to no interest.

The Scripture above recommends you send your grains across the seas, and in time, profits will flow. In essence, it is recommended that you widen your scope across industries and territories. It is expected that you start small and grow it; it assures you that with time and chance, profits will flow back to you.

Finally, it advocates strongly that you divide your investments, which means you do not warehouse all your money in what you may consider a guaranteed investment pot. You do not know what risks lie ahead. A mentor of mine, Apostle Arome Osayi, has said, "There is no security under heaven; there are just opportunities." This is why I am persuaded it is important to diversify investments.

If you choose to avoid debt by the farthest stretch, you must grow your wealth through investments little by little; therefore, be patient. Remember what Proverbs 13:11 (ESV) says on this,

> *"Wealth gained hastily will dwindle,*
> *but whoever gathers little by little will increase."*

Grow your investment in bits and start today!

CHAPTER 8

CONCLUSION

will like you to recite this powerful creed by Max Lucado, a pastor and New York Times best-selling author:

"I will get through this. It won't be painless.
It won't be quick, But God will use this mess for
my good. In the meantime, I won't be foolish or
naïve, and I won't despair either. With God's
help, I will get through this."

The words of this creed brought me untold calmness through many nights especially when uttered with sincerity and from the inner recesses of the soul.

You must understand it takes more than wishful words, but you must constantly utter faith-filled words about your anticipated freedom—of being debt-free. Such powerful confessions send a powerful signal to every fiber of your being and also have a way of putting all that surrounds you on high alert to work in your favour. This confession reveals the real desires of what you carry inside your bowels.

Mark 11:23 (KJV) *"... whosever shall say unto this mountain, be thou removed, be thou cast into the sea; and shall not doubt in his heart but shall believe that those things which he saith shall come to pass, he shall have whatsoever he saith"* (that, my dear reader, includes freedom from the leprous hands of debt!)

Our words have power over our circumstances, and if all you speak about is the overwhelming size of your debt mountain, you will struggle to overcome it. Each word will push the ominous peak closer to the clouds. But if you speak positive words regardless of their size, they will start to shrink, lose ground, and grow smaller. Until one day you will wake up and realize it is gone, totally!

So, learn to weaken the slimy grip of debt by making bold declarations of your imminent victory. Don't let your words, no matter how dire the situation is, become a snare that constricts your possibilities.

Proverbs 6:2 (KJV):

*"Thou art snared with the words of thy mouth,
thou art taken with the words of thy mouth"*

As I conclude what happens to be my debt chronicles, it is important that you understand that you may be struggling with debt or, even worse, cycles of debt, but it doesn't define you, nor is it all you are. YOU TOO CAN BE DEBT-FREE!

I was once reading the UCB Daily devotional when the story below about the apostle Paul sprang to life:

> *"The ship Paul was sailing on to Rome*
> *was wrecked by a storm named Euroclydon,*
> *meaning typhoon, tempest, or cyclone.*
> *Here are some valuable lessons we can learn*
> *from his experience, and which I believe*
> *can be analogous to getting out of your*
> *own Euroclydon debt."*

It is very possible that God can make a bad debt situation work for your benefit. This I have seen happen, and I am a living and breathing testimony of how a rose can grow out of concrete. Because of this shipwreck, Paul ended up on Malta, where the people heard the gospel for the first time. Your debt journey could take you to places where your tales to men will be a liberator.

Sometimes your debt problem can provide a platform for God to work in ways that will amaze you. Your future is not, nor ever will be, in the hands of people. It is solely in God's hands, and what He owns, He protects and provides for.

To reach your God-ordained destination, you will have to sail through storms. I had to sail through the debt storm, and Paul said,

*"All hope that we would
be saved was finally given up."*
(Acts 27:20, NKJV)

*"There will be days when you wonder
how you are going to make it,
but by God's grace you will."*
(Psalm 37:34)

You are the sum total of your choices and must choose wisely moving forward, and in those hard times, you will discover the strength of your connection to God.

The day you wake up after becoming debt-free may seem so far-fetched or attainable, but there is a guarantee that if you follow the steps in previous chapters, not only will you be free from its clutches, you may realize that debt may not appear at the moment, but it may well turn out to be the best thing to happen to you.

Tough processes help to break us down, revealing the real us. This is because strain and pressure will reveal character. There are amazing lessons to be learned along the way that will see you through life's sojourn. Remember that with debt; what may be happening may not just be happening to you; but for you, your perspective is so important.

You might ask, what about those I have lost, Chris? What's next? I lost friends and acquaintances due to my cycles of debts too. So, I want you to know that of all those friends and all those who left you, some may return, and many probably won't. But life makes a provision; it is my belief that it has a self-installed resetting mechanism when it comes to human relationships. With over 8 billion people on the planet, when life sees that you have become a better version of yourself, learnt the lessons for the new season, it will magnetize you to another layer of new relationships. This time, make up your mind not to mess it up.

A major step to be undertaken is to rebuild your self-esteem, and this will not happen overnight. Washington Irving, the American short story writer, famously remarked, "Little minds are tamed and subdued by misfortune, but great minds rise above it." You must rise above your circumstances. You can turn from a laughing stock to a positive reference point. Take a look at your mobile phone; it, like most devices, possesses the ability to erase all past information loaded in it, and you can restore it back to the factory settings regardless of what the previous user has done with it. That's exactly the same ability you possess: to press the reset button, to erase the errors, mistakes, shame, ridicule and the ability to start over.

During those dark days, two of the best pieces of advice I received came from a close friend, and these would help me after the last creditor was paid. These two pieces of advice were:

- The humility to forgive others who had "hurt me" and, most importantly, to forgive myself. At the time when she mentioned this, it sounded offhanded but when I embraced it, I had such a healing experience that would hand me the keys of freedom. Because as you would discover paying the last dime would set you free from others but may not necessarily free you from yourself. Learning to forgive and let go was surely the hardest part.

- The second piece of advice were intentionality and consciousness to be a blessing to others. While this was equally strange, it carried with it, an amazing power to unleash the forces of events and people to work in your favor. This is why debt fights generosity, a call given by God Himself, because Luke 8:18 MSG declares generosity begets generosity. In Matthew 5:42, NIV, it says we should give to those who ask and don't turn away those who want to borrow. Proverbs 11:25 says a generous man will prosper; he who refreshes others will himself be refreshed.

My goal in this book for anyone blessed enough to come across it is to give you my own impression on how you can overcome debt and to create a Karman line between you and debt (the Karman line is the internationally recognized boundary of space which lies around 100 kilometers above mean sea level) – that's the minimum distance between you and slavery. Normally, it is said that it is difficult to build and easy to tear down. With debt, however, it's the other way around. Most of the time, it is very easy to build and extremely difficult to tear it down.

Again, remember, you can be redeemed. Mistakes and debt don't define you if you don't let them. There is a silver lining in every dark, gloomy cloud of debt, no matter how big or dark or how long it hovers in the sky of your life. Although you may have a past, remember that every debtor also has a future.

Debt is a choice, and so is freedom from debt. Today, you can choose if you want to become a lender or a borrower.

Debt subsumes your identity and gives you a new persona, but with the freedom comes a new chapter for you to recreate yourself and your identity. Many successful individuals we celebrate today had their bouts with debt, and their yesterday's trials have become today's testimonies of overcoming the odds.

While writing this chapter, I was hit with a bout of chicken pox, and I was really worried about the nasty swellings over my body. I thought they were going to be a permanent feature of my appearance, but just like debt, a few weeks after it passed, the scabs became scars. I can barely see those boils or faintly recollect the huge discomfort I faced. That's exactly how debt works. Soon enough, after it is gone, all you will have is a few scars to remind you not to return to the past, but more importantly, a life you can truly be proud of.

In Leviticus 25, at the end of each fifty-year period, Israel practiced a special national debt cancellation called the Jubilee, where creditors cancelled all debts and returned all properties to their original owners. Remember, you too can be debt-free and have your own jubilee celebration, and you don't need to wait 50 years; yours can begin today.

Your debt-free partner in success,

Chris Omoijiade

PRAYERS FOR DEBT
& SALVATION

*I am passionate about my love for Jesus Christ,
and I know the role maybe partly of the supernatural in
becoming debt-free. If you are in debt or in any state
of financial difficulty, do you mind if we pray together
for the grace to overcome what I know is a difficult and
demanding season of any person's life?*

PRAYER FOR DEBT FREEDOM

Lord, please forgive me for my past mistakes, and past bad decisions. Provide for me the resources and wealth to remove all the debt and live a peaceful and economically viable life. Let me live the rest of my life under your blessing. I place my heart and my whole life in your hand. Please guide my mind and heart to work on the needy areas and overcome all the fear and stress I am going through. Please grant me peace and abundance instantly in Jesus' name.

By the love and faith in the Lord Jesus, I pray that God eliminates all the past curses, lousy energy, and laziness blocking my financial growth, and I ask you, faithful God, to let my life flourish abundantly. AMEN

PRAYER FOR SALVATION

I know the importance of your body, soul, and spirit being aligned with the purposes of Jesus Christ. As a matter of fact, many of us would never have been in debt in the first instance if we allowed the Holy Spirit to direct the affairs of our lives. You may be just like me, who tried it in his own strength and failed. You have a golden opportunity to become a child of God and receive the grace to execute the steps in this book.

2 Corinthians 4:16 was a Scripture reference I held on to. It is full of so much hope that is practically unsinkable and uplifting; thus,

"Therefore, we do not lose heart. Though outwardly we are wasting away, yet inwardly we are being renewed day by day. For our light and momentary troubles are achieving for us an eternal glory that far outweighs them all. So, we fix our eyes not on what is seen, but what is unseen, since what is seen is temporary, but what is seen is eternal."

Despite the present challenges, even after debt is paid, are you ready for eternity? If your answer is no or you are unsure, let's pray together.

Lord Jesus, I confess my sins and ask for your forgiveness. Please come into my heart as my Lord and Savior. Take complete control of my life and help me to walk in your footsteps daily, by the power of the Holy Spirit. Thank you, Lord, for saving me and for answering my prayer in Jesus' name.

Allow me to be the first to say congratulations, and welcome to the kingdom of light.

THE AUTHOR

Chris Omoijiade, affectionately known as the CEO, is a dynamic figure whose multifaceted talents have left an indelible mark across diverse professional spheres. As an entrepreneur, engaging speaker, dedicated mentor, insightful coach, and innovative consultant, and minister, Chris' passion for teaching leadership and personal success principles has been the driving force behind his illustrious career.

He serves as the Chief Storyteller and Executive at TCOC Global, a boutique consulting firm dedicated to implementing effective tools for enhancing the value proposition and productivity of individuals and businesses. With over two decades of experience, Chris has conducted impactful trainings for prestigious entities such as Continental RE, Diamonds and Pearls, Etisalat, the Nigerian Army, Zapphaire Events, Corona Schools, and Wole Olanipekun & Co., among others, both in Nigeria and Internationally.

Chris' expertise spans management consulting, corporate training, and legal services. He earned himself a Bachelor of Laws degree from the University of Lagos and a Master of Law in Telecommunications and Maritime Law from the University of Hertfordshire, UK. His skill set includes leadership coaching, personal effectiveness, success principles, strategic planning, people management consultancy, and emotional intelligence, catering to diverse clients locally and internationally.

In addition to his professional pursuits, Chris is a minister and a proud graduate of the Koinonia School of Ministry in Abuja. He holds a diploma in Theology and Ministry from the Remnants Christian Network-Adullam in Makurdi, Benue state. Active in esteemed professional bodies like the Nigerian Bar Association, International Bar Association, Institute of Directors, and Chartered Institute of Arbitrators, Chris is dedicated to both professional and spiritual growth.

Chris' literary contributions include insightful books such as 'Get Ahead: Practical Steps to Face Realities and Embrace Success,' 'Gatekeepers,' and the recently concluded 'You Too Can Be Debt Free.' This latest work stands as a testament to Chris' personal journey as a debt survivor, reflecting his passionate commitment to empowering others in their financial freedom and journey into becoming the wealthy man whom God has designed them to be.

As the pioneer of Arimathea Believers Network, Chris envisions a ministry that raises and empowers apostles in the marketplace to seek and fulfill God's will. His desire to unleash the authority and power of God within the marketplace underscores his commitment to righteous apostles influencing and transforming the business landscape.

Happily married with two sons, Chris calls Lagos, Nigeria, home. His unwavering commitment to professional excellence and holistic development is evident in his active involvement in various professional associations, where he continues to contribute his expertise and leadership.

To book Chris for your speaking engagements, consulting, company keynote addresses, trainings, and for ministrations, you can use any of the channels below:

- +234 908 123 0000
- admin@tcocglobal.com
- Chris@chrisomoijiade.com
- Ceo@tcocglobal.com

Follow on social media

- chrisomoijiade
- chrisomoijiade
- @tcocglobal
- @arimathea_believers_network
- chrisomoijiade
- christopher Omoijiade
- The Chris Omoijiade Company
- www.chrisomoijiade.com
- www.tcocglobal.com
- www.arimatheanetwork.org
- comoijiade